C000163163

The Official Guide to Effective Teaching and Learning in Hairdressing

Jane Goldsbro and Elaine White

CENGAGE
Learning

Australia • Brazil • Japan • Korea • Mexico • Singapore • Spain • United Kingdom • United States

CENGAGE
Learning®

The Official Guide to Effective Teaching and Learning in Hairdressing
Jane Goldsbro and Elaine White

Publishing Director: Linden Harris

Commissioning Editor: Lucy Mills

Development Editor: Claire Napoli

Production Editor: Beverley Copland

Production Controller: Eyvett Davis

Marketing Manager: Lauren Mottram

Typesetter: MPS Limited

Cover design: HCT Creative

© 2013 Cengage Learning EMEA

ALL RIGHTS RESERVED. No part of this work covered by the copyright herein may be reproduced, transmitted, stored or used in any form or by any means graphic, electronic, or mechanical, including but not limited to photocopying, recording, scanning, digitizing, taping, Web distribution, information networks, or information storage and retrieval systems, except as permitted under Section 107 or 108 of the 1976 United States Copyright Act, or applicable copyright law of another jurisdiction, without the prior written permission of the publisher.

While the publisher has taken all reasonable care in the preparation of this book, the publisher makes no representation, express or implied, with regard to the accuracy of the information contained in this book and cannot accept any legal responsibility or liability for any errors or omissions from the book or the consequences thereof.

Products and services that are referred to in this book may be either trademarks and/or registered trademarks of their respective owners. The publishers and author/s make no claim to these trademarks. The publisher does not endorse, and accepts no responsibility or liability for, incorrect or defamatory content contained in hyperlinked material.

For product information and technology assistance, contact: **emea.info@cengage.com.**

For permission to use material from this text or product, and for permission queries, email emea.permissions@cengage.com.

British Library Cataloguing-in-Publication Data
A catalogue record for this book is available from the British Library.

ISBN: 978-1-4080-7266-0

Cengage Learning EMEA
Cheriton House, North Way, Andover, Hampshire, SP10 5BE, United Kingdom

Cengage Learning products are represented in Canada by Nelson Education Ltd.

For your lifelong learning solutions, visit
www.cengage.co.uk

Purchase your next print book, e-book or e-chapter at
www.cengagebrain.com

Printed in China by RR Donnelley
1 2 3 4 5 6 7 8 9 10–15 14 13

Elaine White

For Graham, with love, who first encouraged me to teach.

And, for Jake, Leo and Oliver, three amazing boys, with love.

Jane Goldsbro

For Alan, thank you for all your support and encouragement over the years, without it I would never have started writing technical books.

Brief contents

Contents

Introduction

There has never been greater focus on teaching, learning and assessment than there is now. Judgements made about the effectiveness of teaching, learning and assessment, in its widest sense, is a critical part of all government inspections.

This book has been developed following the outcomes of numerous observations of teaching and learning as well as training sessions provided for teachers of hairdressing. The ideas within the book have been tried and tested by teachers who can measure an improvement in their learners' understanding. And importantly, the same teachers have raised their own motivation, self-fulfilment and confidence when teaching.

Within the book you will see that the learning experience is likened to a good, satisfying and enticing meal. Imagine going into a restaurant and every time you went in, the exact same meal was served to you. You would soon become bored and disinterested. You would know what you were to be served before starting your meal. Likewise, if you constantly serve up the same teaching and learning experience to your learners, they too will become complacent as they will know exactly what to expect, even before they enter your classroom. But, by using the ideas in the book and varying your teaching and learning strategies and methods, you can introduce a planned element of surprise in all your sessions, which will keep your learners interested and engaged, and thus improve their learning.

Like any skill, teaching is something that needs to be practised and refined. As with practitioners in many occupations, teachers can never say they know it all. There is always something new to learn, and it is this that makes teaching so rewarding. There is always a fresh challenge to master or an untried technique to conquer. It is not possible to change the way you teach overnight, but it is possible, over a period of time to gradually introduce new strategies and methods that will enhance the experience for all learners.

When you are confident in your own teaching skills, the observation process, whether by peers, colleagues or government inspectors, becomes a great opportunity for your learners to demonstrate, that through your teaching skills they learn well, both independently and by collaboration with others. And in addition they make good progress relative to their starting points and produce work that exceeds the requirements of their qualification.

So, you may be a new teacher looking for advice and guidance about how to develop your techniques. You may be an experienced teacher in a rut using the same, safe, tried and tested teaching strategies and methods. Or, you might simply be looking for more innovative ways to enhance teaching and learning. In any of these cases, this book should provide a helpful framework to support you with the delivery of new and engaging methods to improve the learning experience for all your learners.

About the website

A wide range of online materials, from lesson plan templates to learning activities accompany this book.

All materials relating to learning activities are based at level 2. The content of the materials can easily be *simplified* for learners working at level 1 or entry level, or *amplified* to provide more challenge for learners working at level 3.

To access this wide range of teaching support materials and templates follow these simple steps:

1) Visit www.cengagebrain.co.uk and search for the *The Official Guide to Effective Teaching and Learning in Hairdressing* ISBN 9781408072660.

2) Click on the Free Study Tools Link.

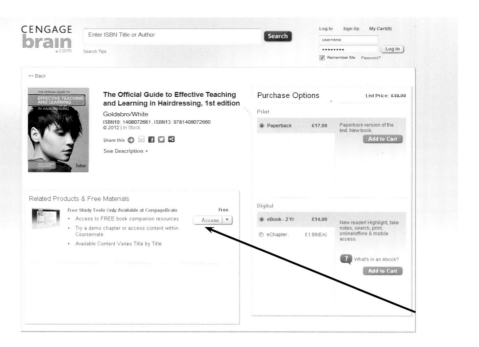

Acknowledgements

Jane Goldsbro and Elaine White would like to thank Claire Napoli for her assistance and support during the publication of this book and Lucy Mills for taking up the original concept. Their thanks also go to Alan Goldsbro and Graham White for all their valuable help.

Our thanks go to the teaching team at Nottingham Hairdressing Training Agency for testing many of the teaching and learning ideas included in this publication. In addition, thanks to the directors and managers of Nottingham Hairdressing Training Agency for their kind permission to use the template for the lesson plan and the document for integrating critical aspects into the hairdressing curriculum.

Grateful thanks also go to Justine Drury of Tiger Solutions for sharing her ideas for the go-around (dialogue) cup and the great wall of ideas, to Laura Fern for the suggestion for the QR Code treasure hunt and to the wider teaching community everywhere who freely share their amazingly creative ideas.

For providing images for the book, our thanks go to Graham White.

Text and image credit list

CREDITS

Although every effort has been made to contact copyright holders prior to publication, this has not always been possible. If notified, the publisher will undertake to rectify any errors or omissions at the earliest opportunity.

Images, Figures and Tables:

The publisher would like to thank the following sources for permission to reproduce their copyright protected images, figures and tables:

Atherton J S (Learning and Teaching; Conversational learning theory; Pask and Laurillard, 2011) 95b; **Honey & Mumford** (The Manual of Learning Styles, Peter Honey Publications, 1986) 39b; **Professor David Kolb** (Experimental Learning Cycle) 40t; **Shannon and Weaver** (The Mathematical Theory of Communication, 1949) 2b; **Shutterstock** – pp 4b, 9t, 11c, 14b, 18t, 22t, 24t, 29b, 31c, 33m, 42b, 44t, 50b, 52b, 54c, 61t, 65b, 69t, 73b, 76c, 78c, 83m, 85c, 91m, 93t, 97b, 109c, 113t, 118t, 125t, 130m, 139b, 143b, 151t, 158m; **Graham White** – pp 71t (The Cutting Book, 2007), 158t, 159t; (Adapted from http://ww2.odu.edu/educ/roverbau/Bloom/blooms_taxonomy.htm) 56b

About the authors

Elaine White

Elaine White has a lifetime of experience in the hair and beauty sector. She has been involved with the development and implementation of some of the most influential hair and beauty programmes in colleges, schools and in work-based learning.

Throughout her career, Elaine has been involved in researching the processes and developing systems that have raised standards in the hair and beauty sector. She has contributed massively to hair and beauty education, the standards for which are renowned throughout the world. Her passion for learning and development has taken her from the hair and beauty industry into the challenging world of further and higher education. Here she spent more than 16 years as an educator before joining Habia, the Standard Setting Body for the hair and beauty sector.

Her role with Habia allowed Elaine to work with a diverse range of stakeholders from schools and colleges to learning providers and universities to develop and introduce innovative learning programmes, apprenticeships and foundation degrees. One of her most rewarding projects was to research the incidence of dyslexia in the hairdressing industry. This project culminated in presenting the findings to an invited audience at the House of Lords, the home of the upper chamber of the UK parliament.

Elaine continues to provide support and expertise to learning providers as an educational consultant for quality improvements in teaching, learning and assessment. She is also a technical author with four published books supporting hair and beauty qualifications. And, she is a moderator and examiner for hair and beauty qualifications.

Jane Goldsbro

A qualified hairdresser since 1982, Jane is one of the most influential educators in hair and beauty today. Her skills in developing the structure of UK hair and beauty education are renowned throughout the world.

Jane's early career as a hairdresser took her through a formative path where she ran salons and worked for some of the best companies and key influencers in the field of education such as Alan International, and at Redken worked as one of their top technicians.

At an early stage of her career, Jane was a regional winner of the L'Oréal Colour Trophy at the tender age of 17 whilst still training at North Lindsey College; this led her to start a teaching career at North Lindsey. However, the deep rooted commitment to continue learning saw Jane taking on her biggest challenge when she went to work at Habia.

1992 saw Jane start at Habia as Development Manager for Hairdressing and within four years Jane had risen to Director of Standards and Qualifications. This role saw her take on bigger challenges each and every year. Not only did Jane enhance the development of hairdressing education, she began to expand Habia's remit into Beauty Therapy. Since those heady days of endless development meetings, running standards workshops and training international educators in Habia techniques, Jane has still found time to develop her skills.

An established writer of technical material for Habia, Jane is also the author of two hairdressing study guides and four hairdressing text books, including The Official Guides to the Diploma in Hair and Beauty Studies for both the Foundation and Higher levels, on behalf of Cengage Learning, the leading publisher in hair and beauty. Her expertise in training and assessing has enabled her to work with and support all the hair and beauty awarding organizations in the UK in the development of qualifications.

Her role at Habia as Director of Standards and Qualifications now covers all six sectors of Habia's portfolio in hair, beauty, nails, spa, barbering and African-type hair. She is responsible for setting the standard for hair and beauty education from schools to university graduates in the UK and with our international partners in Spain, Italy, Japan, China, Malta, India, Syria and USA.

Truly, one of the most knowledgeable hair and beauty educators in the world.

About the book

The Official Guide to Effective Teaching and Learning in Hairdressing relates to the delivery of teaching and learning for any hairdressing qualification. There are six chapters in the book, each of them covering, in a logical format, an aspect of any learning session from communicating, right through to evaluation.

Features within the chapters

Quotes

Each of the six chapters begins with an inspiring and motivating quote related to the content of the chapter.

> *I am still learning.*
>
> *Michelangelo (1475–1564) artist, sculptor, architect and engineer*

Introduction

The introduction outlines the context for the chapter.

INTRODUCTION

This chapter covers the importance of effective curriculum and lesson planning both from the teacher and learner perspective. It is recognized that there are as many different ways of planning teaching and learning as there are learning providers. However, the focus of the chapter is what should be included within the planning process. The chapter will include the purpose and rationale for planning, how to plan and what to plan.

Chapter learning objectives

The learning objectives are stated in each of the chapters. They outline what you can expect to have learned by the end of the chapter.

CHAPTER LEARNING OBJECTIVES

This chapter will support the development of:

- Enhanced knowledge of the planning process for teaching and learning
- Effective curriculum planning
- Effective lesson planning
- Self-evaluation for the completion of chapter objectives

Important note

Critical aspects of text have been highlighted along with helpful tips and guidance for teaching and learning.

Important note

The hairdressing industry is creative, it is all about fashion, and it is very important that your professional appearance reflects that expected by the industry.

Online reference document

A wide range of materials from lesson plan templates to learning activities can be downloaded from: the Effective Teaching and Learning resource website.

All materials relating to learning activities are based at level 2. The content of the materials can easily be *simplified* for learners working at level 1 or entry level, or *amplified* to provide more challenge for learners working at level 3.

Online reference document

You can download a document from *the Effective Teaching and Learning resource website: Chapter 1* which provides further examples of how Bloom's Taxonomy can be used to develop understanding by the use of persuasive speech.

Research activity

The authors have highlighted opportunities where you might wish to investigate an aspect of teaching and learning in more depth. These activities will frequently link with the content or tasks and assignments included in teacher training qualifications, or for the development of effective learning materials.

 RESEARCH ACTIVITY

Discuss with others about how you would put The Mathematical Theory of Communication into practice for your own teaching delivery.

Web box

The authors have researched useful websites that will support your development for teaching and learning.

Web box

Further information on safeguarding can be found at:
   www.education.gov.uk.

Development checklist

At the end of each chapter you will find a development checklist in which you can measure your own progress related to the content of the chapter. By using the checklist you can develop an action plan to identify any support or training you might need to further develop your own skills for teaching and learning.

Development checklist

Visit the *Effective Teaching and Learning resource website* to download a development checklist summarizing what you have covered in Chapter 2.

CHAPTER 1

Introduction to teaching and learning in the hairdressing industry

Communication – the human connection – is the key to personal and career success.

Paul J. Meyer 1928–2009 Founder of Success Motivation International

INTRODUCTION

This chapter covers the importance of communication in teaching and learning within the hairdressing industry. It is recognized that an important aspect of teaching and learning is being able to communicate effectively to everyone in the learning environment to ensure a motivational learning experience. In the chapter you will look at different forms of communication, how to create a positive, professional learning or working environment that reflects the conditions that are required within the hairdressing industry, and the importance of good mentoring skills. The chapter will also include the requirements of continuing professional development.

CHAPTER LEARNING OBJECTIVES

This chapter will support the development of:

....

- Enhanced understanding of communication skills
- Effective learning environments
- Effective mentoring
- Self evaluation of your performance and continuing professional development needs

The ***Wikipedia dictionary*** defines communication as:

The process of transferring information from a sender to a receiver with the use of a medium in which the communicated information is understood by both the sender and receiver.

Communication skills for teachers

Teaching and learning is much more than just imparting knowledge to learners. Teaching and learning is about effective communication to people of all ages, backgrounds and starting points. When effective communication is missing, teachers can misunderstand their learners' needs and expectations; furthermore learners may not feel listened to or understood and then disengage from the learning process.

Teaching can be considered as 50 per cent knowledge and 50 per cent interpersonal or communication skills.

 RESEARCH ACTIVITY

The diagram below was developed by Claude Shannon and Warren Weaver (1949). The Mathematical Theory of Communication was used to explain how communication occurs. Research their theory and discuss how this approach to communication can be used in the learning environment.

Figure 1.1   The Mathematical Theory of Communication

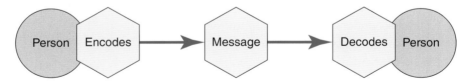

Web box

You can use the links below to help in your research:

http://www3.alcatel-lucent.com/bstj/vol27-1948/articles/bstj27-3-379.pdf.

RESEARCH ACTIVITY

Discuss with others about how you would put The Mathematical Theory of Communication into practice for your own teaching delivery.

Effective communication keeps the mind open to learning. A good teacher will use all forms of communication, verbal and non-verbal, as well as listening skills during each teaching and learning session to enhance the learning process.

Keeping the mind open to learning will ensure that:

- Learners will cooperate
- Learners feel involved and understood
- Both you and your learners feel listened to
- Potential conflicts can be resolved
- You understand your learners' needs
- Learners understand your needs
- Learners build confidence and self esteem
- You have mutual respect
- Everyone is interested and gets value out of the lesson

It is worth noting that, just because you have said or written something, it does not automatically mean that the learner has received it or understood it. There are many skills required when communicating and it is down to you to choose the right method to ensure your message is delivered and understood.

Consider some of the following communication skills required by teachers:

Speaking	The ability to express messages simply and clearly
Listening	The ability to listen to what is being said
Understanding	The ability to comprehend what has been said or written

Reading	The ability to understand written information
Discussing	Sharing information
Negotiating	Sharing information, putting your point of view across in an open discussion to compromise on a situation so that both sides are in agreement and you achieve a 'win–win' situation
Networking	The ability to work in groups, share ideas and contribute to discussions
Empathizing	The ability to understand how someone is feeling, and be able to share those emotions
Persuading	The ability to reason with or convince others about your beliefs
Assertiveness	The ability to be confident and forceful

Verbal communication

The person sending information has to express all of their feelings, needs, wants, dreams, hopes, values, beliefs and thoughts using understandable language within the message.

The person receiving the message has to be able to listen to the information, decipher it, understand all that has been communicated, and then act upon it. This means that if one party gets the communication process wrong, then the information fails to be delivered or carried out correctly.

The way you send a message can make a huge difference when using verbal communication. The way your voice sounds and the speed at which you speak will have a huge impact on how the message you are trying to put across is actually received by your learners.

Think about the:

- Tone
- Pitch
- Volume
- Timbre
- Speed
- Sense of humour, enthusiasm and motivation...

that you interject into your voice when giving information and how you would like your learners to react to what you are saying.

Using your voice

Your voice is one of your key assets in getting information across to learners. Speak in a normal, conversational tone and use appropriate hand gestures. Because you are speaking to a group of people, you may need to use more volume, more vocal variety and more emphasis to get your message across. As you get more experienced you will learn to use more effective methods of using your voice and gestures.

Remember the following tips:

- Speak at a moderate speed and enunciate your words clearly.
- Voice moderation is important. Do not speak in a monotone; use effective conversational inflections.
- Make sure you know and use the correct pronunciations of all terms you are using within the lesson.

- Speak from the diaphragm and not the throat. Your voice will carry better and you are less likely to sound nervous.
- Use appropriate hand gestures for emphasis during your lesson, but do not overdo it or make them too wild, as it can be distracting.
- You do not have to speak continually; build in pauses or ask questions to make sure the learners are still with you and you have their attention.
- Try not to use verbal pause fillers such as 'okay', 'you know' and 'alright'. With practice, you will stop using them.
- Do not read your notes, you can make your points more effectively and keep your learners' attention by speaking directly to them.
- Do not teach sitting down, as your voice comes from the throat. By standing up you can control your breathing and present a strong visual authority.

Persuasive speech

Persuasive speech is a communication approach used to influence learners to accept a particular position.

Use *persuasive speech* to take learners through the five stages of understanding:

1 Explaining the problem.
2 Understanding the problem.
3 Understanding the proposed solution.
4 Visualizing the effect of the proposed solution.
5 Understanding how they must act or react.

Important note

The five stages of persuasive speech link with one of the most widely known learning domains – Bloom's Taxonomy. You will find a research activity relating to Bloom's Taxonomy in Chapter 3.

Bloom categorizes learning activities into knowledge, skills and attitudes. In each category Bloom describes how learning begins with the simplest forms of knowledge, skills, or attitude. Then, from the simplest form of learning activity, each category can be developed into the most complex aspects of knowledge, skills and attitudes. The same can be said for the effectiveness of persuasive speech.

An applied example of persuasive speech would be how to influence learners to have an empathetic approach when dealing with a client found to have head lice.

1 **Explaining the problem** – this relates to the *recall* of knowledge. The learner must know the facts about head lice to accurately inform the client about the problem.

2 **Understanding the problem** – this relates to the *comprehension* of knowledge. The learner must be able to answer client questions about head lice.

3 **Understanding the proposed solution** – this relates to the *application* of knowledge. The learner must be able to advise the client about a solution for the problem.

4 **Visualizing the effect of the proposed solution** – this relates to the *synthesis* (creativity) of knowledge. The learner must be able to see beyond the problem and think creatively – after all you want to retain, not lose the client.

5 **Understanding how a stylist must act or react** – this relates to the *evaluation* of knowledge. The learner must be able to critically evaluate how they dealt with the problem and if necessary, improve their approach.

Online reference document

You can download a document from *the Effective Teaching and Learning resource website: Chapter 1* which provides further examples of how Bloom's Taxonomy can be used to develop understanding by the use of persuasive speech.

Informative speech

First tell them what you're going to tell them, then you tell them. Then you tell them what you told them.

(Rafe, 1990)

Informative speech is the main form of transmitting information about, for example, the structure of the skin, or the hair growth cycle. Constant use of *informative speech* is often disengaging for learners, therefore you need to be creative and use multi-sense learning, interlaced with informative speech techniques to maintain the learners' interest.

Listening skills

This is truly one of the most important communication skills that you need to use for teaching and learning. While hearing is an activity that requires little physical effort, to do it properly is hard work. Listening is not easy and you need to concentrate on the person that is giving you both verbal and non-verbal information so that you can receive and translate that information.

As a teacher you will use listening skills, not only in the lesson to respond to questions, but also in learner reviews to capture and identify any hint of problems the learner may have, but is unwilling to openly tell you about without careful prompting.

When using listening skills with learners you demonstrate a:

● Desire to understand how the learner is thinking or feeling

● Belief and interest in the learner

● Respect of the learner

● Desire to help, explore problems and help the learner to understand possible choices and consequences

● Willingness not to be judgemental

Incorporating discussion groups and role-play activities within a lesson can enhance your learners' listening skills. In the hairdressing industry it is vital that listening skills are developed to ensure that stylists clearly understand their clients' wishes so that they can deliver the exact requirements of the client.

Reflective listening

Reflective listening is a key ingredient in communication. It is used to confirm the meaning of what is being said by repeating back what you think you have heard. You are then able to demonstrate that you have accurately understood what has been said. This method is very useful to ensure you understand problems, potential conflicts, or misunderstandings.

The use of open questions will invite learners to talk more and direct their attention to a specific aspect. Open questions, which start with words such as; 'how', or 'tell me about' relate to the lower level thinking skills, which depend on the recall of knowledge. Questions that start with; 'why' relate to higher level thinking skills, which some learners may find more difficult to respond to.

Important note

It is important to use differentiated questioning techniques to both support learners and for further development. You will find further information about the effective use of questioning and assessment for learning in Chapter 5. For example, by using extending questioning techniques, an open question can be used to focus on the problem a learner may have. With support, the learner can be directed to think more about what's gone wrong and focus on the solution. Thus, supporting the learner by effective questioning from the recall of knowledge, through to the application of knowledge and eventually to the evaluation of knowledge.

Non-verbal communication

Although learners will take in information from communication, a large amount of information is absorbed through non-verbal methods.

It is important to ensure that the verbal and non-verbal messages that you are giving are the same. If they are contradictory, there may be confusion. Therefore, the non-verbal messages of body language, attitude and dress are all critical to the whole information package that you are delivering as part of your lesson. As a teacher you need to be able to read your learners' body language and mannerisms. You need to be flexible and capable of changing your communication strategy if you are losing the impact of the message you are trying to send.

Body language accounts for approximately 50 per cent of the information you want to give your learners. Your tone of voice will be approximately 40 per cent of the information received and the words you use will make up the remaining 10 per cent.

Being able to understand body language and interpreting the signs and acting on them will help create a good teaching and learning experience.

Getting to know your learners

When you are new to teaching it can be quite daunting to deliver a teaching session. It is common to feel anxious, nervous, or excited, but everyone gets stage fright at some time in their life. Use these feelings to your advantage; instead of being scared that you might make a mistake or not connect with the learners, think about the lesson as an opportunity to present your knowledge and ideas through effective learning. Remember, your learners want you and expect you to support them well. They are attending your lesson with the expectation of being informed about the subject they are interested in, through the support of a knowledgeable, enthusiastic teacher, with the expectation that they will succeed.

When you first meet your learners, you are entering into a relationship with them that could last for a long period of time.

Remember, first impressions count. In the first few minutes of meeting someone, we will make a decision about them, even if this is, or is not, an accurate impression. When a learner enters the room for the first time, they will survey their surroundings and look at you as the teacher. You need to ensure that it is a positive first impression.

Your learners may vary from group to group. Typical groups in hairdressing for example could be:

- 14–16 year old learners working on school link programmes.
- Learners participating in an apprenticeship.
- Learners taking a full time, college-based hairdressing qualification.
- Adult learners wanting a change of career or catching up on missed opportunities.
- Unemployed learners, trying to re-enter the world of work.
- A qualified hairdresser wanting to improve their current skills.

It is your role to break down any barriers to learning and to build a calm, trusting environment in which learners feel comfortable and confident to absorb new information.

Remember:

- A calm and confident attitude will put the learners at ease.
- A relaxed learner is usually more attentive.
- Appreciate your learners, extending them courtesy.
- A cheerful and humorous attitude engages learners and gives them a sense of accessibility.

However, understanding the importance of a calm attitude and having one are two different things. How can you achieve this when you are nervous, your knees are knocking and your hands are sweating?

Here are a few ideas:

- Take your time to prepare your lesson. Remember, *'fail to prepare, prepare to fail'*.
- Practise, practise, practise is your best defence for combating nervousness. It is vital that you know your subject well and what you are going to deliver in the lesson.
- Act confident, even if you don't feel confident.
- Assume a positive stance with your feet shoulder-width apart and your weight evenly distributed.
- Take slow even breaths, breathe evenly from your stomach.
- If your hands are shaking avoid using them; focus on the subject you are delivering and not on your hands – the shaking will stop.
- If you feel that you are losing control, stop talking and take a few deep breaths. It will give you time to collect your thoughts and refocus yourself on the subject you are delivering.
- Have a sense of humour – you'll need it.

Evaluate the effectiveness of your classroom management when delivering your lesson. Get feedback from your learners and use it. Survey your learners as you are delivering the lesson. Check for signs of interest, boredom or hostility from learners.

- Do learners look relaxed and attentive? Do they have open posture: arms open, hands relaxed. Or do they have a closed posture: arms crossed, fists clenched? Are they looking at you, reading or looking out of the window? Are they disengaged or being disruptive?
- Do they look confused? If they do not understand some part of the lesson, learners will often discuss a point with each other, rather than ask the teacher. Some learners will tentatively raise their hand, so that they can ask you to explain. If you are observing the learners while you are talking you will see these signs and you can stop and ask if they need anything explaining further.
- If the non-verbal cues you are identifying from the learners mean that you are not getting your message across, you will need to be responsive and modify your delivery method. For example, you may need to change the modulation of your voice, or use a different method of delivery that involves more learner participation.

Appearance and body language

The nature of the environment in which you are going to present will often dictate how you will appear. If, for instance, you were speaking at a formal evening presentation, it would be assumed that you would wear formal dress, to complement the occasion and the audience.

Plan how you want to appear, and think about the message your appearance will make. This will depend on the environment you are teaching in. In hairdressing, for example, you may be teaching in a classroom, lecture theatre, or a realistic learning or working environment.

These environments may dictate what you wear, from casual clothes to a uniform, but it is important that you set the scene for the environment that you want to create for the learners. Ask yourself, will my appearance enhance the message I am giving or distract my learners from hearing the message?

Not only does what you wear have an impact on the message you want to send but also your posture is important in conveying an assured presence. Make sure that you give a confident but relaxed message. Stand up straight, weight evenly distributed on both feet, with hands relaxed at your side. The way you stand, make eye contact and use your facial expressions will all give a message to your learners about you, your confidence, your attitude and belief in what you are teaching.

- A genuine smile lights up your face and conveys happiness and interest.
- Eye contact lets people know that you are listening and interested.
- Your head tilted to one side will indicate that you are interested.

Whereas:

- Standing with hands on hips can give the impression of aggression or frustration.
- Crossing your arms can make you appear defensive.
- Touching your face can indicate anxiety.
- Clenching your fists can indicate tension or aggression.

Important note

Remember, teaching is a skill that needs to be practised. What works in one situation may not work in another lesson. Try things out, go with your instincts and what feels right, have confidence in your ability to adapt to different environments or circumstances and accept that you may not get it exactly right every time.

Important note

The hairdressing industry is creative, it is all about fashion, and it is very important that your professional appearance reflects that expected by the industry.

Environment

The environment can really affect the way communication is taken and understood. The way the room is organized, be it a classroom or realistic working environment, the colour, temperature, ventilation, noise and smells will all affect communication. The environment can have both a positive and negative effect on you and your learners. As part of your lesson planning make sure that the environment that you will be using is conducive to the learning process.

Culture

Being aware of different cultures and not assuming that everyone is the same will give you a greater understanding of people and communication skills. Culture can refer to religion, social, political and family customs. Different cultures have different perceptions on many issues, such as personal comfort zones. Everyone communicates differently and it is down to you as the teacher to make the learning environment effective for all your learners to feel safe, comfortable and inspired.

Cross cultural communication

Culture is about human expression. It involves the behaviours, beliefs and practices of individuals and their communities. Cross cultural communication requires an understanding of different cultures. If you do not have an understanding then how do you effectively communicate to someone who understands and relates to the world differently from you? Effective communication with people of different cultures is challenging. Cultures provide people with a way of thinking, seeing, hearing and interpreting the world. The same words can mean different things to people of different cultures. People of the same culture but living in different parts of the same country can also have different interpretations to teaching and learning, even when they speak the same language.

Each culture has its own rules about behaviour that affects verbal and non-verbal communication.

This can include:

- Whether to use eye to eye contact.
- Whether to say directly what you mean or talk around the issue – for example, in the Japanese culture you would not use negative words like 'no', you would use positive words to explain the problem or why something could not happen.
- How close you should stand next to someone.

As you are finding out, communication is a complex process, but very important to your success as a teacher. The communication process can be broken down into six main components and it is up to you to choose not only the information you want to send but also the personal impression you want to make. You must assess your learners and decide how best to reach them both verbally and non-verbally.

Six communication components

1 Sender of information – the teacher.

2 Channels – senses: speech, hearing, seeing, touching.

3 Message – the learning topic.

4 Receivers – the learners.

5 Noise – internal and external factors that affect what the learners hear.

6 Feedback – learning outcomes.

Professionalism in the learning environment

As a teacher your professionalism will affect your learners' ability to learn effectively. Professionalism can be defined as the ability to reach your learners in a meaningful way, by developing innovative ways of delivering your lesson to ensure sessions are motivating, engaging and inspiring to your learners. By doing this you are reducing the risk of having to deal with disruptive learners during your lessons.

Think of professionalism as containing three main characteristics:

- Competence – knowing your subject area
- Performance – how you deliver information
- Conduct – your behaviour

Competence

Competence is vital to your success as a teacher. Competence will include preparation and knowledge of your subject area.

Preparation will include *lesson plans*, the set up of the learning environment and knowing your learners, from language and cultural barriers to socio-economic differences. All teachers face issues in the classroom that need to be considered and prepared for, to ensure individual needs are identified and dealt with as part of your overall preparation to create an effective learning environment.

A teacher with strong knowledge and experience of their subject will have more opportunity to prepare innovative teaching materials rather than spend time reviewing or learning the subject area they are about to teach. In understanding your subject well you will have more confidence and are more likely to deliver a well-planned and interesting teaching and learning session.

Performance

Although competence is vital to your professionalism, it is only useful if you can perform the role of an effective teacher. Performance is the ability to effectively pass on relevant information to the audience in such a way that all your communication skills are used to actively engage all learners, taking a real interest in their progress.

Conduct

Finally, and equally as important, is conduct. Conduct is a representation of how well you present yourself to others and covers appearance, language and personal behaviour, and will reflect on how you are perceived by learners. All these aspects break down to one important component – effective communication skills.

Overall professionalism is a combination of different aspects, it covers far more than the notion that a teacher is there to provide information. Below is a quick summary of what being a professional means:

- Preparing yourself, your learning environment and your material.
- Being able to cope with a range of teaching and learning situations.
- Being able to adapt to different situations.
- Quick thinking and flexibility to meet the emerging needs of learners.
- Understanding your learners and their cultural differences.
- Knowing your subject.
- Being innovative in your teaching, learning strategies and methods.
- Not becoming too familiar with your learners and keeping a professional distance.

Important note

Although you want to build a good relationship with your learners it is not a good idea to connect with your learners through social media or to give your learners your private mobile phone number.

Safeguarding for children and learners

Safeguarding is an area that is a high priority for Government and all learning provision, be it a school, college or private training provider.

Government inspections will review internal procedures to ensure they are effective and that the implementation of policies and routines involves every member of the learning provision.

The definition of safeguarding can be summarized as:

- Protecting children and learners from maltreatment.
- Preventing impairment of childrens' and learners' health and development.
- Ensuring that children and learners are growing up in circumstances consistent with the provision of safe and effective care.
- Undertaking the role so as to enable those children and learners to have optimum life chances and to enter adulthood successfully.

Reference: The Children Act 2004 Working together to Safeguard children – Department for Education and Skills (now DfE) guidance document, 2006.

Two main inspection issues follow from this definition:

1 The effectiveness of settings and services in taking responsible steps to ensure that children and learners are safe.

2 The effectiveness of settings and services in helping to ensure that children and learners feel safe.

The list below highlights some of the key features of outstanding practice:

- High-quality leadership and management that makes safeguarding a priority across all aspects of learning.
- Stringent vetting procedures in place for staff and other adults.
- Rigorous safeguarding policies and procedures in place, written in plain English, compliant with statutory requirements and updated regularly; in particular, clear and coherent child protection policies.
- Child protection arrangements that are accessible to everyone, so that learners and families, as well as adults in the school, know who they can talk to if they are worried.
- Excellent communication systems with up-to-date information that can be accessed and shared by those who need it.
- A high priority given to training in safeguarding, generally going beyond basic requirements, extending expertise widely and building internal capacity.
- Robust arrangements for site security, understood and applied by staff and pupils.
- A *curriculum* that is flexible, relevant and engages learners' interest; that is used to promote safeguarding, not least through teaching learners how to stay safe, how to protect themselves from harm and how to take responsibility for their own and others' safety.
- Courteous and responsible behaviour by the learners, enabling everyone to feel secure and well-protected.
- Well thought out and workable day-to-day arrangements to protect and promote learners' health and safety.
- Rigorous monitoring of absence, with timely and appropriate follow-up, to ensure that learners attend regularly.

- Risk assessment taken seriously and used to good effect in promoting safety.

Reference: Ofsted Safeguarding Best Practice, 2011

As a teacher dealing with different age groups it is important that, wherever possible, safeguarding is incorporated within your lessons to ensure learners recognize dangers and harmful situations and know the preventative actions they can take to keep themselves safe. This is particularly important for children and young adults wanting to work in a customer-focused industry, such as hairdressing. They will be working in environments that contain sharp tools, electrical equipment, chemicals and clients, and it is important that they are taught skills that they will need for adult life and the working environment, alongside their mental, emotional and physical well-being.

Learners need to be aware of their responsibilities in relation to behaviour and the expectations of the teacher for learners. This may involve a code of conduct that reflects safeguarding requirements and the needs of the hairdressing industry. Learners also need to understand and accept the consequences for any misdemeanours.

Web box

Further information on safeguarding can be found at:
   www.education.gov.uk.

Dealing with learner disruptions

Even if you are a good teacher and you have planned everything to enable you to deliver a professional and enjoyable lesson, there may be occasions when a learner has a barrier to learning.

Sometimes a learner's previous experience to learning will create a barrier that will prevent learning from taking place; this could interrupt other learners, resulting in disengaged learners. Often barriers to learning are due to learners' lack of confidence, lack of basic skills, lack of understanding for what is expected of them, or simply that they are struggling to adapt from a previous learning environment to a new adult learning environment.

In hairdressing there is a higher proportion of learners with *dyslexia*. If this has not been identified during their previous learning experience, it can often create a barrier to learning. Carrying out effective initial and ongoing *assessment* will help identify a learner with dyslexia as well as other barriers to learning.

Not all these barriers can be broken down by good communication skills. Your professionalism as a teacher and the principle of a learner-centred approach when designing your lessons will help. Learners may need additional support through preparatory sessions, preparing the learner for learning, learning to take place at a level and pace relevant to their needs, targeted and supported learning and structured tutorials or mentoring.

Important note

As a teacher you should never be afraid of asking your peers for help or advice. Even the most experienced teachers can struggle in some classroom situations.

Mentoring and being mentored

A mentor is someone who helps another person through an aspect of their life such as a new job, a qualification, or in career or personal development. This support is commonly used for new teachers. The person being mentored is called the mentee. Mentoring is a relationship in which learning and *experiential learning* occurs through analysis, practice and reflection on situations, problems, mistakes and successes to identify learning opportunities. Mentoring is about helping mentees to grow in self-confidence, independence, autonomy and maturity.

Mentoring only works when the two people involved make a real connection that is built on trust, respect, openness and honesty. In the early stages of the process the mentee will be relatively dependent on the mentor, who needs to be supportive, helpful, friendly and nurturing. As the mentee becomes more confident the mentor will need to challenge and stimulate the mentee. The aim is for both parties to contribute freely to the process so that they operate as equals.

The traditional form of mentoring is one to one mentoring but there are other forms such as peer mentoring and group mentoring.

As a new teacher, having a mentor is a helpful way of enabling you to consolidate your skills and have guidance and support in order to develop competence and confidence in your teaching skills.

Within education mentoring is an effective way of supporting learning, to secure understanding and to bring about personal change.

Mentoring is characterized as being:

- Focused on supporting the mentee's personal effectiveness
- A long term, one to one relationship based on trust and interpersonal skills
- A mixture of creating challenge and giving support

It has a number of functions that include supporting personalized learning by reviewing the mentee's progress, development and effectiveness, as well as advising and guiding mentees on qualification choices, reviewing attendance, mentee engagement and well-being.

Online reference document

Download further information on the benefits of mentoring and being mentored from *the Effective Teaching and Learning resource website: Chapter 1*.

Continuing professional development requirements for hairdressing

To have a professional career as a hairdressing teacher you will need to have appropriate qualifications or be working towards them. As a hairdressing teacher it is not only important to have a teaching qualification, you will also be required to carry out continuing professional development (CPD) to update your skills for teaching.

It is vital to ensure you have credible, up to date technical hairdressing skills and knowledge to ensure you give a good impression and confidence to hairdressing employers that you have contact with, and your learners. Each Sector Skills Council (SSC) may require assessors and verifiers to undergo industry-specific continuing professional development requirements in addition to those set for teaching. In hairdressing, Habia, the Standards Setting Body for the Hairdressing Industry, sets CPD requirements in their NVQ/SVQ assessment strategy, to ensure a minimum of thirty hours technical updating per year is completed for full-time assessors and verifiers delivering 'job ready' qualifications. This will be pro-rata for assessors or verifiers that work part-time. These hours will need to be recorded and will be verified by the awarding organization.

Habia has not developed an assessment strategy for vocational qualifications, also known as 'preparation for work' qualifications, although it is seen as good practice to carry out hairdressing CPD, no matter which hairdressing qualification is being delivered.

Web box
....
Further information on hairdressing CPD requirements can be found in the Sector's NVQ Assessment Strategy at www.habia.org.

 RESEARCH ACTIVITY
....

Download the Habia Assessment Strategy from their website. Find out about the different types of technical hairdressing CPD that is required. Then, plan the type of CPD that you would like to undertake to increase your technical skill or knowledge to benefit you and your learners. This activity could be taken one step further by discussing your plans with your mentor.

Development checklist

Visit *the Effective Teaching and Learning resource website* to download a development checklist summarizing what you have covered in Chapter 1.

CHAPTER 2
How learners learn

I am still learning.

Michelangelo (1475–1564) artist, sculptor, architect and engineer

INTRODUCTION

This chapter provides an overview of different learning theories and *preferred learning* styles. Over several centuries, psychologists have tried to define how learning occurs and there are many different and varied views. Basing lesson planning on the theory and principles that underpin how learners learn will ensure that you are able to adopt the most effective way for session delivery. Not all learners learn in the same way, or at the same time. Some learn best by doing, some by watching, while others prefer a logical, step-by-step approach as a way of gaining skills and knowledge. Because of this variation, it is useful to identify preferred learning styles. Sometimes there may be barriers to learning which may be related to social, psychological or physical needs. However, common barriers to learning are directly related to individual learning needs. This chapter will look at one such learning need; dyslexia. Knowing how your learners learn will assist in the development of individualized teaching and learning techniques, devised with the appropriate levels of support, to meet the needs and interests of all learners.

CHAPTER LEARNING OBJECTIVES

This chapter will support the development of:

....

- Enhanced knowledge of a range of learning theories
- Application of the learning theories in programme planning
- Identification of preferred learning styles
- Increased awareness of effective teaching and learning for those with dyslexia

Learning theories

Historically, over numerous decades, psychologists have identified many different categories of learning theories. The theories each have their own distinct characteristics and are clearly different. Yet, the diverse theories should not be viewed in isolation. While there are marked differences, and often opposing views, there are also similarities and a degree of overlap between each of the theories. Furthermore, for each of the theories, there are different theorists, each with their own unique perspective on the exact, same theory.

Some of the main theories of learning include:

- *Behaviourism*
- *Cognitivism*
- *Constructivism*
- *Humanism*

School of psychology	Simplified concept	Application	Theorists
Behaviourism	That learning is the achievement of new behaviours. Learning is regularly rewarded to reinforce further learning and to increase motivation. Without reinforcement learning can be forgotten. Teachers respond to learning by rewarding learners with positive	Delivery of new topics in small bite-sized pieces where constant reinforcement of learning and timely reward for success can be initiated. Ensure the learning outcomes are very clear, achievable and measurable.	Skinner Pavlov Watson

School of psychology	Simplified concept	Application	Theorists
	reinforcement when the desired learning outcome has been achieved.		
Cognitivism	Learning is about thinking, the development of intellectual skills, the thought process and the storing and retrieval of information that is derived from prior knowledge. Learning takes place when learners are taught how to do something through guidance and an explanation of knowledge using a step by step approach in which they are actively involved.	Delivery of new topics by building from simple to more complex aspects of knowledge. Start with prior knowledge and encourage learners to state facts they already know. Support development with clear explanations through step by step, active learning.	Gestalt psychology Anderson Vygotsky
Constructivism	New information or concepts are computed and connected to existing information or concepts. Learning occurs when learners are able to reflect on	Delivery of facilitated guiding of new ways to solve problems. Allow learners to construct their own knowledge through self-directed learning, in groups or on their own. Be	Piaget Dewey Bruner

School of psychology	Simplified concept	Application	Theorists
	their own knowledge and gain new understanding by building 'constructs'. Learners add additional knowledge to their existing knowledge, thereby creating a deeper understanding.	aware that the constructs that learners make may not be correct, so effective feedback is required to check learning.	
Humanism	Self-motivating approach to learning. Allowing learners a degree of choice and where they can be empowered and take responsibility for their own learning.	Delivery of individualized learning where the learner is able to have some measure of influence to negotiate and choose what and how they learn. Use of active learning for the development of self-discovery. Learners can use self-assessment to identify and use their strengths to compensate for any areas of weakness.	Maslow Rogers Kolb

Applying the theories

As with any good teaching and learning session, planning should be based on how your learners will learn best. Using a diverse range of activities is more likely to ensure that learners are actively engaged and interested. Think about this when planning your learning session and plan your activities in line with the different theories about how learners learn.

For example, you could use all the theories that have been outlined above in one way or another to cover the learning topic of haircutting. The lesson, incorporating the identified theories, would include effective client consultation, followed by a practical activity to cut hair.

Using the theory of behaviourism

The theory is that learning is the achievement of new behaviours or knowledge. Learning is regularly rewarded to reinforce further learning and to increase motivation. Praise, reward and constructive, timely feedback to learners are all crucial for motivation and for progression through the learning programme. Sometimes you could use more tangible incentives to reward learning behaviour, for example, certificates, badges or prizes.

Applied example of behaviourism

Activities to promote a behaviourist approach need an element of reward. You could, for example, provide a short text related to the critical influencing factors that affect the choice of cutting techniques. Then, ask learners to read the text. Next, give the learners a short period of time for them to think of some questions that might 'puzzle the teacher'. This part of the activity can be completed as paired work and thinking of the questions to ask will help to develop higher-level thinking skills. Learners should be rewarded with appropriate praise when identifying questions for the teacher to answer. Follow this with teacher-led questions that might 'puzzle the learner'. Questions that are answered correctly are rewarded. The reward is positive and immediate praise and feedback. Feedback itself is very gratifying, particularly when using a rewarding praise word that learners personally like to hear. You can use words learners like to hear by using the 'go around cup' technique.

Important note

It has to be noted that learners who have difficulty in answering questions may find this kind of activity worrying. To avoid this, prepare individualized and differentiated questions, so learners of all abilities are able to positively respond.

Online reference document

You can download the relevant text to develop a behaviourist activity from *the Effective Teaching and Learning resource website: Chapter 2.*

Online reference document

You can download the instructions and information about making and using the *'go around cup'* from *the Effective Teaching and Learning resource website: Chapter 2.*

 ## RESEARCH ACTIVITY

Develop a learning activity which can be delivered in short, bite-sized pieces, and in which each piece of learning can be rewarded with positive reinforcement. Investigate how your learners like to be rewarded. Some may like praise, others more tangible incentives, such as bonus points that lead to celebratory awards. Gather feedback from your learners about the effectiveness of the activity. Share your work with colleagues as an example of good practice.

Using the theory of cognitivism

Learning is about thinking, the development of intellectual skills, the thought process and the storing and retrieval of information that is derived from prior knowledge. To achieve learning outcomes, learners not only have to learn the information, they need to be able to store information and retrieve it at crucial times. They can only do this if the knowledge is part of their long-term memory. For effective reinforcement, it is helpful to spread learning over a period of time, rather than to teach once and then never to refer to the subject again. Learners need to rehearse and practise their knowledge to place it into their long-term memory.

Applied example of cognitivism

To support the retention of information held in the learner's long-term memory, try to develop activities that include an element of recall practice. You can do this by ensuring that the activity integrates with and links new knowledge with existing knowledge. Creating such links will assist recollection of information. Active problem solving learning will support the cognitivist approach. For example, a game based on dominos can be used to remind learners about the consultation terms they may use in haircutting. This step by step game will help to store and reinforce relevant words into the long-term memory. By using the game, learners will be able to provide a rationale for the placement of their domino tile. This rationale will confirm (or not) their understanding of the consultation terms.

Online reference document

You can download the relevant resources to develop a domino game for cutting consultation from *the Effective Teaching and Learning resource website: Chapter 2.*

 RESEARCH ACTIVITY

In relation to Gestalt psychologies, you may have heard the saying *'the whole is greater than the sum of its parts'*. For example, in relation to the temporary changes in the hair structure during styling hair, learners need to be aware of (a) the hair structure, (b) the physical changes that occur when heat or water is applied to hair and (c) the different ways the hair can be moulded and manipulated to change the natural shape. Because learners need to understand how all these separate elements come together, the process of cohesive setting is greater than the sum of its individual parts. Find other examples and plan how you can ensure effective learning of individual parts, linking them to the 'whole' picture.

Using the theory of constructivism

New information or concepts are computed and connected to existing information or concepts. Learning occurs when learners are able to reflect on their own existing knowledge and gain new understanding by building 'constructs' related to the new knowledge. They connect together new and previous learning, thereby creating a deeper understanding. It is important to note that learners have to make the constructs themselves. It cannot be done by their teacher, but it is the role of the teacher to facilitate the learning experience.

Important note

The constructs learners make may not always be correct. Therefore, effective feedback techniques are required to check and confirm learning.

Applied example of constructivism

Using a constructivism approach to teaching and learning means that you must enable learning, rather than teach. Learners must be able to make connections from their previous learning, constructing new learning by themselves. Typically learners will be actively engaged in problem solving. They will be able to discuss and debate their new learning by making reflective connections to previous learning. An example of how this learning theory can be applied and linked, in this case to consultation for haircutting, would be through consultation case studies. Learners will be able to transfer the knowledge of general consultation findings and 'construct' links from generic information to that directly required for cutting hair.

Online reference document

You can download the relevant case study resources to apply a constructivist approach to learning from *the Effective Teaching and Learning resource website: Chapter 2.*

 ## RESEARCH ACTIVITY

You can see a very interesting lecture about constructivism on the website for the Institute for Learning, led by Geoff Petty: http://vimeo.com/42685056. Watch the lecture and then, when introducing a new learning topic, develop an activity which will enable learners to make effective constructs.

Using the theory of humanism

The theory supports the notion that learners are self-motivating and driven to learn. For this approach to be most effective learners must be allowed a degree of choice of what and how they learn, following identification of their own strengths and areas for improvement. This can be achieved by taking into account their previous learning and results of their initial, ongoing and self-assessment. By doing this, learners are empowered and enabled to take responsibility for their own learning. In addition, learning will be individualized and focused on self-directed discovery.

Important note

Humanism is often associated with adult learners, but all learners can benefit from a degree of facilitated independence.

Applied example of humanism

An example of how a humanist approach can be used for teaching and learning could, in relation to haircutting, be delivered by using a range of hairstyle images for learners to interpret and then later, plan, apply and reflect on their skills. To try this approach, provide images of finished looks for learners. These can be in case study form that can be completed on modelling blocks, or on live models. Allow learners the freedom to choose a hairstyle they wish to complete. Facilitate and support learners to complete a consultation to determine the techniques required to complete the haircut. Learners should be encouraged to plan, apply skills, reflect on their progress and then propose and plan how to improve the first outcome.

Online reference document

You can download the relevant case study resources and images from *the Effective Teaching and Learning resource website: Chapter 2.*

RESEARCH ACTIVITY

There are many more and different learning psychologies, which include:

- **Theories of memory and intelligence** – such as Howard Gardner's theory of multiple intelligences.
- **Andragogical** – such as Malcolm Knowles' theories related to adult learning.
- **Design theories** – bridging the gap between theory and practice.
- **Social learning theories** – role of social intervention on learning and development.

Investigate these and other theories and see how you might plan for and link learning experiences.

Web box

One useful website with an explanation of a vast range of theories, including those listed above, can be found here:
http://www.instructionaldesign.org/theories/index.html.

Preferred learning

A great deal of research has been carried out to investigate how learners prefer to learn. For example, some research has identified different *learning* styles, such as visual, auditory, reading/writing and kinaesthetic learning. Others see learning as a *learning* cycle. For example, learners plan and complete a task. Then, following a review of the task, they apply the improvements they have identified. Some research is about how learners' learning relates to the way the left and right side of the brain compute information, and other research focuses on a 'whole brain' approach.

In all cases, it is recognized that while there may be a preference for one style or another, we all benefit by developing the styles of learning that may not be our first choice. After all, we would not be doing any favours to learners by restricting learning development.

> **Important note**
>
> *Using a variety of learning strategies and methods will ensure that learners have the opportunity to learn about a given topic using different skills. This will further develop individual learning in a style that learners prefer. And, importantly, it will support development of learning styles learners find more difficult.*

Using learning styles to plan effective teaching and learning

Knowing the way learners prefer to learn is a very useful start for planning effective teaching and learning. By delivering information in a style that both appeals and relates to the learner it is more likely to be memorable, and memorable learning is more likely to be recalled. Learning styles can be identified by using a wide range of questionnaires in which learners can identify how they learn best. From this self-assessed information a profile can be formulated and, importantly, shared with the learner. The profile will outline the preferred learning style and the typical characteristics that make up the learning style.

Web box

Geoff Petty's website has a range of questionnaires that can be used to identify a variety of different teaching and learning styles. Look at his site http://www.geoffpetty.com/style.html and see how you best match the ways your learners prefer to learn with the methods you use to facilitate learning.

Important note

It is important that the information related to the preferred learning style is used carefully. There is little evidence to suggest that focusing entirely on one preferred learning style will lead to successful learning. At the same time, there is not much point in presenting learning in a style which does not engage the learner. So, while it is useful to identify a preferred learning style which can be used as a starting point for lesson planning, the best learning occurs when a variety of learning styles are used. By doing so, a multi-sensory approach to teaching and learning can be developed.

Learning styles

While research suggests that teachers should not place too much importance on learning styles as the sole basis for lesson planning, it is useful to know about some of the preferred learning styles. Recognizing a range of different learning styles will certainly support the development of varied and interesting approaches for the delivery of topics.

VARK

One of the most commonly identified learning styles is **v**isual, **a**uditory, **r**eading and **k**inaesthetic, or *VARK*. This means that some people prefer to learn visually, by looking. Some prefer to listen, some to read/write and some by physically doing a task. However, to support learning development, all hairdressers need to refine their ability to visualize, to listen, to read and to do a range of tasks. The way information is taught helps learners to understand. Therefore, effective teaching and learning will occur when all these learning styles are supported.

Applying VARK

You could plan your lesson to cater for all types of preferred learning styles within the VARK range. For example, when teaching how to cut hair, you can combine the four preferred learning styles by:

Visual Showing a DVD of the relevant haircut and demonstrating how the haircut is completed.

Aural   Explaining the principles of the haircut and giving step by step explanations.

Reading   Asking learners to read about the haircut in their course textbook to confirm the correct methods, and complete a head profile handout by drawing the required angles for the haircut.

Kinaesthetic Allowing learners to complete the haircut on a block or live model.

You could carry out a demonstration, clearly explaining the relevant points to learners. This will support learners who like to watch and those who prefer to listen to instructions. While listening, auditory learners and those who like to read and write may like to take a few key notes relating to instructions, check facts in a text book and complete a handout illustrating the angles required for the haircut. Visual learning can be supported further by showing an appropriate DVD. In addition, as visual learners learn best by seeing things, studying images and diagrams, they could watch the DVD at the same time as referring to images in their text book. Then facilitated kinaesthetic learning will occur when the learners actually carry out the haircut, thus supporting the learning style of learners that like to learn through movement.

A method of combining all four preferred styles in a practical training session simultaneously could be achieved by having access to an electronic tablet or mobile device with an appropriate app, which is placed on the workstation. Then, as the learners are practising their skills, they could rerun, watch, read instructions and listen to the app at points that are critical to their individual requirements for understanding.

Web box

The VARK learning styles are widely known and commonly identified. Investigate the VARK learning style, which includes how learners may prefer learning through reading, by completing the questionnaire on this website: http://www. vark-learn.com/english/index.asp or http://www.wsc.ac.uk/vark/questionnaire.asp.

RESEARCH ACTIVITY

Download the Chapter 2 lesson plan activity from *the Effective Teaching and Learning resource website: Chapter 2* and complete the task to identify where the learning theories of behaviourism, cognitivism, constructivism and humanism are planned for application in the learning session. Then, using the same lesson plan, identify where the preferred learning styles of visual, aural, reading/writing and kinaesthetic are covered by the tasks in the lesson plan. On completion of the task, discuss your findings with peers.

Experiential learning

As the name suggests, experiential learning is learning by experience. This type of learning allows learners to acquire new skills by doing things, and to learn from their mistakes. To be successful, learners also need skills to be able to self-evaluate their experience or performance and to draw critical conclusions that will enable them to apply new, improved learning.

Activist, reflector, theorist and pragmatist are four learning styles identified in 1986 by Alan Honey and Peter Mumford. The underpinning principles related to the Honey and Mumford learning styles stem from the work of David Kolb and his experiential learning theory.

Honey and Mumford learning styles

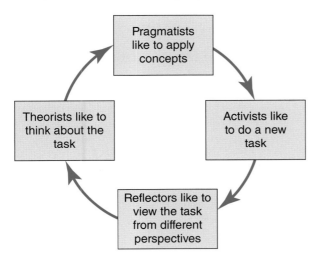

Kolb's experiential learning cycle

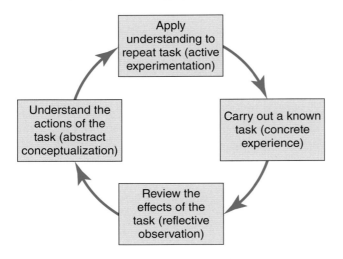

Honey and Mumford	David Kolb
Activists Like to be involved in doing things	**Concrete experience** Carry out a known task
Reflectors Like to review their learning before drawing conclusions	**Reflective observation** Reflect on the task
Theorists Like to think about problems in a logical, step by step way	**Abstract conceptualization** Critically analyze work
Pragmatists Like to try out new techniques	**Active experimentation** Test and implement new ideas

Important note

When using experiential learning, it is important to provide learners with sufficient support to make the learning experience a positive one.

Applying experiential learning

Memorable activities will enable enhanced recall of skills for future, improved application.

For example, (1) learners could carry out a cutting technique on a modelling block or live model by applying existing skills. They would then, (2) reflect on the results of the haircut using self-evaluation techniques. Then, by (3) critically analyzing their work and taking account of how the task was carried out, they can build on their previous learning. Finally, the learner will be able to (4) apply the information they have gathered from their reflective and critical evaluation to repeat the task to improve learning, or transfer their skills to another task.

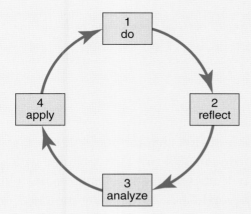

Kolb describes this cycle as a continuous spiral. He suggests that although the starting point can begin anywhere within the cycle, the value of the theory is that learning is a continuous process of development. Likewise, Honey and Mumford state that while learners may prefer one of the learning styles within the cycle they have identified, they should have the opportunity for exposure to all learning styles to develop weaker areas.

Important note

By moving through the experiential learning cycle, learners can experience a range of different learning styles to deepen and improve their understanding of knowledge and tasks.

RESEARCH ACTIVITY

Investigate more about Kolb's experiential learning cycle and Honey and Mumford's learning styles. Use the theories to develop a learning activity in which learners are able to carry out a task, then reflect and analyze the outcomes to apply new, improved skills. Alternatively, you could extend the exercise for the Chapter 2 lesson plan activity by identifying where experiential learning is taking place.

Web box

....

Information about the downloadable Honey and Mumford questionnaire can be
found on this website:
http://www.peterhoney.com.

Web box

....

More about David Kolb's theories and critiques of these theories can be found on
this website:
http://www.reviewing.co.uk/research/experiential.learning.htm#axzz20blzu9d6.

Multiple Intelligences

....

If you have read the opening section of this chapter you will see that
multiple intelligences (Howard Gardner 1983) are also included as a
learning theory. Gardner would say that multiple intelligences are not
the same as learning *styles*. But, nevertheless, by drawing on the
learning abilities identified by Gardner, educators found it is possible
to recognize the differences in the *ways* that learners like to learn.

Gardner recognized that not everyone can learn in the same way. All
learners have different strengths, therefore they cannot be taught in
exactly the same way. He demonstrates evidence to support the notion
that unless learners take an active part in their learning, then learning
will not be remembered.

Gardner identified seven separate intelligences, then later added an eighth and lately, a ninth.

Online reference document

Download the Gardner intelligences table from *the Effective Teaching and Learning resource website: Chapter 2* to see how the separate intelligences can be easily applied in a hairdressing context.

Applying Gardner's separate intelligences for hairdressing

Web box

There are a range of tests freely available on the Internet to identify which of your multiple intelligences are strongest. By asking learners to complete the tests, a profile is generated indicating how they might learn best and will provide useful information to support learning.

http://psychology.about.com/library/quiz/bl-mi-quiz.htm

http://www.bgfl.org/bgfl/custom/resources_ftp/client_ftp/ks3/ict/multiple_int/index.htm.

Impact of learning psychologies and learning styles

By using a range of holistic methods of *initial assessment* you can identify appropriate teaching and learning strategies to engage with and support your learners. It is very useful to know *how* learners learn and how they *prefer* to learn. In theory, by doing this, you will support individualized learning designed to connect and engage with learners. However, while it is possible to exactly tailor learning for individual learners on a one to one basis, it is almost impossible to do this for all the individual learners in the whole group. Therefore, by creating and facilitating learning sessions using an appropriate mixture of all the learning theories and styles, all learners will enjoy learning in their preferred style, while unconsciously developing and strengthening skills they may otherwise ignore.

Web box

....

More about the impact of learning styles can be found on this website:
  http://archive.excellencegateway.org.uk/page.aspx?o=152477.

Dyslexia in the hairdressing industry

Dyslexia is a particular issue for some learners, as research has shown a higher incidence of this condition amongst hairdressers. Research by Habia, the standard setting body for the hair and beauty sector, found that the incidence of dyslexia in the hairdressing industry is twice that you would expect to find in the population as whole.

Many dyslexics are often highly intelligent and very creative people. They are frequently artistic and are good with the style of verbal communication required for acting and debating. Coincidentally, these skills are also necessary for a successful hairdressing career. The creative nature of hairdressing, as well as the often misguided notion that it is wholly a practical subject, means that it is an attractive occupational option for those with dyslexia.

Web box

Effective initial assessment can often highlight typical indicators that a learner may have dyslexic tendencies. A work pack of hairdressing-related activities developed by Habia in conjunction with the Adult Dyslexia Association will provide additional and vital information to support learning.
http://www.habia.org/shop/hairdressing-and-barbering/training-support-materials.

What is dyslexia?

Dyslexia is often described as a learning *difference*, rather than a learning *disability*. Recognizing this is very similar to recognizing that all learners, with or without dyslexia, have differences in their learning styles.

But, because of this learning difference, sometimes dyslexia can be a barrier to learning. Those with dyslexia are typically less fluent in reading, writing and spelling, and for some, less fluent with numbers.

While no two people with dyslexia are alike, typical characteristics might include:

- Weaknesses in short term memory.
- Problems with sequencing – placing words or phrases into a logical sequence – such as days of the week.
- Weaknesses in the speed at which information is processed.
- Difficulties in organizing and routine.
- Having low self-esteem.

Teaching and learning for learners with dyslexia

If you have read the first part of this chapter you will know that learners learn best when there is a multi-sensory approach to teaching and learning. This means that you need to use a variety of different teaching and learning strategies and methods to account for differences in learning styles. When you do this, learners, at some point in the learning session, will be learning in their preferred style. At the same time, they will be introduced to other learning styles which will support the development of other less dominant skills.

Important note

By using a multi-sensory approach to learning you can make learning interesting and engaging for all the learners in the group, whatever their learning preference or ability. And, it is a very well recognized fact that learners with dyslexia benefit from this very same approach. So, if you make learning engaging for dyslexics, learning will be engaging for all.

Online reference document

You can download a checklist for teaching and learning that will support learners with dyslexia from *the Effective Teaching and Learning resource website: Chapter 2*. This checklist is based on the recommendations from the British Dyslexia Association for teaching and learning that will support learners with dyslexia.

Web box

The BDA produces an excellent guide to ensure the font size and colour and paper-based resources can be read by those with dyslexia. http://www.bdadyslexia.org.uk/about-dyslexia/further-information/dyslexia-style-guide.html.

For more useful information about dyslexia see:
http://www.bdadyslexia.org.uk/files/DFS%20pack%20English.pdf.

Development checklist

Visit *the Effective Teaching and Learning resource website* to download a development checklist summarizing what you have covered in Chapter 2.

CHAPTER 3
How to plan for teaching and learning in hairdressing

When planning for a year, plant corn. When planning for a decade, plant trees. When planning for life, train and educate people.

Chinese proverb

INTRODUCTION

This chapter covers the importance of effective curriculum and lesson planning both from the teacher and learner perspective. It is recognized that there are as many different ways of planning teaching and learning as there are learning providers. However, the focus of the chapter is what should be included within the planning process. The chapter will include the purpose and rationale for planning, how to plan and what to plan.

CHAPTER LEARNING OBJECTIVES

This chapter will support the development of:

....

- Enhanced knowledge of the planning process for teaching and learning
- Effective curriculum planning
- Effective lesson planning
- Self-evaluation for the completion of chapter objectives

The planning process

With any plan, at the beginning you must be able to identify what the end result is going to be. In the case of teaching and learning, your main aim, and end result, is to facilitate enjoyable and successful learning outcomes that meet the needs and interests of all your learners, as well as the requirements of the qualification.

The journey taken to achieve these aims needs to have:

- A clearly identified beginning
- A structured, yet flexible middle
- An effectively evaluated end of session

Important note

The evaluation at the end of the session ensures that you have useful information about the effectiveness of teaching and learning to plan a new, revised and improved beginning for subsequent sessions.

The beginning, middle and end can relate to both curriculum planning and to lesson planning.

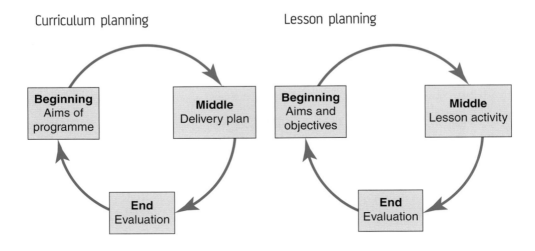

Curriculum planning

Adopting a cycle of continuous development for the curriculum helps to ensure that teaching and learning programmes are fit for purpose and that an opportunity for effective evaluation is available.

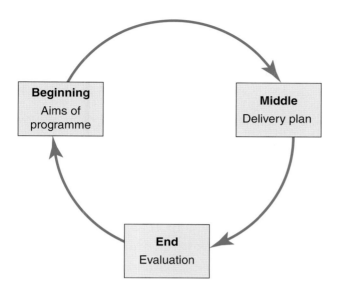

1 The beginning

The beginning of curriculum planning, in which the curriculum aims are identified, should begin with the development of a *scheme of work*. A scheme of work is a working document and is used to plan the long-term, overarching aspects of the curriculum in a logical and coherent order for teaching and learning. Once completed and as it is used, it can be refined and changed to accommodate emerging issues, adaptations for learning needs and to make improvements for future programmes.

However, you can't begin to plan a scheme of work until you know the answers to the following questions:

1 What are the specifications for the learning programme?
2 Who are my learners?
3 What are the assessment requirements of the learning programme?
4 How long does the programme last?
5 How will the programme be taught?
6 What resources are required?

Question 1 What are the specifications for the learning programme?

The *specifications* for the programme may be set by an awarding organization and will lead to a nationally recognized qualification, or be set by the programme deliverer where achievement may not be nationally recognized.

The specifications set by an awarding organization will clearly specify the syllabus or expected learning outcomes by describing them through modules or units related to a particular subject. The specifications will describe the knowledge and if applicable, practical skills that have to be attained before a qualification can be awarded. There will be guidance about the amount of time that should be spent on each unit or module. In addition, many awarding organizations provide direction and support about how the programme can be delivered. The resources required to deliver the programme will be outlined. This can relate to physical resources, for example, working areas, such as for hairdressing, the need for a realistic working environment which replicates a commercial hairdressing salon, and teaching aids. In addition, staff resources and the qualifications, expertise and experience teachers need to have for the delivery of the programme.

Other programmes may be designed by the learning provider and achievement may be recognized by an in-house certificate. However, you will still need to plan for the programme with the same structure and rigour as that required for nationally recognized qualifications.

Important note

One useful aspect of in-house devised programmes is that the views of users can be more easily accommodated in the design of the learning outcomes. In some cases, a programme may be developed in partnership with learners or with employers to ensure their specific learning requests or skill gaps are met.

RESEARCH ACTIVITY

The *Sector Skill Body*, Habia, develops the National *Occupational Standards* for hairdressing. These standards are used for the basis of all nationally recognized qualifications. You can use the same standards to develop in-house devised programmes to develop the skills and knowledge needed for different occupations. They can be used to identify training needs, skill gaps and to support clear career paths.

Download the National Occupational Standards for your learning programmes and refer to them when you are planning your curriculum. If you are not responsible for curriculum planning, download the standards to confirm where the work you are delivering interlinks with other aspects of the curriculum.

Web box

The National Occupational Standards can be downloaded from:
   www.habia.org.uk.

Awarding organizations have set processes for monitoring the internal and external quality procedures for delivery and assessment. This ensures that the delivery and assessment standards are consistent, nationally, across all learning providers. Centre devised qualifications still need to be consistently delivered and assessed to ensure that the learning outcomes achieved are authentic, valid and reliable.

Important note

Whether the learning programme is a nationally recognized qualification, or a centre devised in-house certificate of achievement, quality assurance is paramount.

Question 2 Who are my learners? Planning for the curriculum often has to be completed before you know who will be on the programme itself. Therefore, you cannot account for individual learner characteristics without making stereotypical assumptions about hairdressing learners. This detail will come later, at the lesson planning stage. However you will need to know the general, overarching makeup of your learners; for example, their likely social and cultural background, gender or age.

For example, without making stereotypical assumptions, the approach you may have for the delivery of a programme to 14–16 year olds will be different from that required for the same programme attended by a group of adult learners. This is because adults will have more life experience and are often highly motivated for learning. At the same time, some adults may begin a learning programme with trepidation. They may have had bad experiences at school which has left them with low self-confidence. Furthermore, the learning focus for adults can vary from self-fulfilment to career progression, so you may have a wide variety of learner expectations to plan for.

 RESEARCH ACTIVITY

A leading theorist on adult learning was the American, Malcolm Knowles (1913–1997). His vast research outlines the principles of why and how adults learn. Investigate the theories to support your curriculum planning.

Web box

....

A short, but informative video clip about Malcolm Knowles that summarizes his
theories can be found here: http://www.youtube.com/watch?v=U4iMFu4CnLQ.

Conversely, 14–16 year old learners will be used to the structure of a
school timetable. If attending learning programmes in a more adult
environment, such as a college, they may be unused to an autonomous
learning environment. One other consideration relating to age is that
some programmes may be restricted for those under the age of 16 or
18 because of health and safety or other types of legislation.

You will need to identify if there are any prerequisites for the
programme. Do learners need to have achieved other aspects of learning
before they can begin the programme you are planning, or can they
begin without related learning experiences? You may need to plan for a
variety of different starting points as learners, even with the same entry
level attainment, will each have different learning requirements.

Question 3 What are the assessment requirements for the programme?

Assessment is an important part of the teaching and
learning process. It allows the teacher and the learner to check if the
learning outcomes have been met. Learning programmes will be
assessed formally or informally at the end and/or throughout the
programme. The process, in terms of curriculum planning, is almost
identical for formally and informally assessed programmes. You need to
allow sufficient time to deliver the learning outcomes, and in addition,
to allocate time for assessment, whatever its type. However, the time
allocated will vary according to the specific assessment requirements.

Some formal, summative or *assessment of learning* will be completed
with learners taking an exam on a given day. Therefore, in addition to
planning for the learning outcomes, the *curriculum plan* needs to be
devised to prepare learners for this culminating activity. Other
summative assessment will be ongoing and continuous. In which case,
the curriculum plan will need to be sufficiently flexible to allocate
assessment time for all learners, each of whom may need to be
assessed at different times throughout the programme.

Although also recognized as a *teaching method*, *'assessment for learning'* will be carried out continuously, throughout the entire programme, as will more informal and *formative assessment*. Some form of assessment which provides feedback to the learner about how they have performed and can improve, will take place throughout each individual teaching and learning session and, in some cases at the end of the programme. Therefore, schemes of work must be able to accommodate this.

Important note

A powerful example of formative assessment is assessment for learning. Assessment for learning is a motivating tool for improving learning outcomes. It is a mechanism to combine formative assessment, in which useful information can be gathered about the readiness of the learner to be summatively assessed, and an opportunity for learners to self-assess to test their own understanding and plan where to go next.

Question 4 How long does the programme last? The length of a learning programme will be defined as Guided Learning Hours (GLH). Guided Learning Hours is the term given to describe the time allocated to directed study or assessment led or facilitated by a teacher and completed by a learner. Knowing how long a programme is expected to last provides you with a firm foundation for your scheme of work. It means you can plan from the introduction to the end of the teaching and learning programme. However, not all learners learn at the same speed. Some learn quickly, others may need more time to reflect and revisit topics again. Therefore, the scheme of work needs to have capacity for both revision and extension activities to maintain interest and to ensure the individual needs of all learners can be met.

Question 5 How will the programme be taught? Whatever the learning programme, the teaching and learning strategies and methods used should be appropriate for the learning outcomes, and meet the individual needs of learners. A variety of engaging and interesting activities that can challenge and motivate learners should be planned into the scheme of work. More information on teaching and learning strategies and methods is found in Chapter 4. Some programmes require the constant presence of the teacher, while for others a degree of independent learning is expected. Here, learners will spend time without the teacher, researching and preparing evidence to meet the learning outcomes.

Important note

Curriculum planning should include time for both teacher and learner activity.

Question 6 What resources are required? The programme specifications set by the awarding or developing organization will outline the resources that are required for the programme. The resource requirements for completing a programme will vary depending on the type of qualification. This can be anything from the room in which the qualification is delivered to the tools and equipment that are used by learners. For example, for National Vocational Qualifications which are 'ready for work' qualifications, the resources will have to replicate in a school or college, those found in the industry itself. These learning environments are generally referred to as *'Realistic **Working** Environments'*. For vocational qualifications known as 'preparation for work' qualifications, the learning environment is referred to as a *'Realistic **Learning** Environment'*. This environment will still provide a degree of realism, but the expectations of a commercially-operated business are not required.

Staff resources for the programme need to be carefully planned. The main teacher may want to bring in visiting speakers or teachers with additional and curriculum-enhancing expertise, so the programme may have to fit around their availability.

2 The middle

The middle of the curriculum plan is the development of the content for the planned learning sessions. Effective learning takes place when the easier tasks or knowledge are delivered and completed first, before the more complex skills and theories. Therefore the development of the scheme of work should follow a logical, coherent, step by step approach to learning.

There are many different theories about how learners learn, and which teaching and learning strategies work best. One such and best known example is Bloom's Taxonomy (1956), which describes three different categories of learning activities. The categories are *knowledge, skills* and *attitude*. Each category can be broken down into further subdivisions. In each case the subdivision begins with the learning of the simplest levels of knowledge, skills or attitude. Then, once learners have mastered the more basic elements, more complex aspects of knowledge, skills and attitudes can be developed.

The progression from the simplest form of learning to more complex forms is illustrated on the diagram below.

Bloom's Taxonomy

Create
The learner is able to construct new ideas

Evaluate
The learner is able to make judgements

Analysis
The learner is able to examine and question concepts

Application
The learner is able to use information in a variety of ways

Comprehension
The learner is able to understand and explain different ideas

Knowledge
The learner is able to remember to recall information

Source: adapted from http://ww2.odu.edu/educ/roverbau/Bloom/blooms_taxonomy.htm

RESEARCH ACTIVITY

Download an example extract of a scheme of work for haircutting from *the Effective Teaching and Learning resource website: Chapter 3* and note how the skills and knowledge build from week to week using the principles of Bloom's. Carry out an exercise to identify where each subdivision of Bloom's Taxonomy can be attributed to the skills and knowledge planned for delivery.

RESEARCH ACTIVITY

Investigate Bloom's Taxonomy and apply the principles to your scheme of work. When devising your learning programme, begin with the simplest forms of knowledge, skills and attitudes, and develop learning logically through to the more complex aspects. Effective learning relies on the completion of all the categories, even at the most basic level. During your investigation, note how Bloom's 1956 original classification has been adapted to better represent teaching and learning today.

In addition to building from simple to more complex tasks, you need to ensure that you plan for the coherent and logical introduction of all aspects of the learning programme. Some skills or aspects of knowledge take longer than others to perfect or understand and, despite being more complex, may have to be introduced at an early stage of the programme to allow sufficient time for skill development or understanding, particularly if the learning programme requires competence of skills.

Important note

Remember that the scheme of work is a working document. It can be changed and altered to account for emerging issues and to meet the needs of the learners. Making changes does not mean that the scheme of work was incorrectly developed. On the contrary, it shows that through teaching and learning it was adapted, amended and moulded to meet the emerging needs of the learners.

3 The end

··

When the programme reaches the end, the next and most critical step is evaluation. You need to be able to clearly identify what has worked well and what needs to be changed for the next delivery of the programme. If the scheme of work has been used as a working document, the evaluation will be easy. You will actually have been doing it as you have gone along, and all you have to do is look at the progressive notes you have made.

In addition to your own, a good evaluation will include the views of all users. This means all that have been involved in the design, development and delivery of the programme, as well as those who make judgements about the quality of the programme.

For example:

Learners	Feedback from learners is vital. They will be able to tell you exactly what the content and delivery was like for them. You should be able to confirm (or not) that the needs of all learners have been met through the individualization of the teaching and learning sessions. In addition, you can establish if the length of the programme and delivery sessions were appropriate and then make future plans based on your findings. Judgements about the effectiveness of the learning programme can also be determined by the number of learners that have enjoyed their experience and successfully achieved all their learning aims.
Employers	The views of hairdressing employers are vital for both employer-responsive and learner-responsive programmes. For curriculum development to work well an effective partnership is extremely beneficial. Employers should be consulted to ensure that they

▶

	have the opportunity to comment on and influence training, teaching and learning to meet local and national skill needs and labour demand.
Clients/Consumers/ Customers	The majority of hairdressing programmes require the cooperation of a loyal and flexible range of clients to provide the commercial and real life experience for learners. Feedback on the design and delivery of the programme will support sustainable consumer relationships.
Parents/Carers/ Guardians	Some hairdressing programmes may have required the support of parents, carers or guardians. For example, school link programmes may require cooperation for transport to the centre or outside activities. Financial contributions may have been required to assist with running costs of the programme, or for programme enrichment.
Schools	Their views are important for the coherent and coordinated delivery of a programme which may include several partnerships within a consortium.
Awarding organizations	External verifiers or moderators will provide confirmation that the programme has met national requirements in terms of quality assurance. If not, they will provide an action plan that must be implemented. You need to review the overall success of the programme. Exam and qualification success rates will confirm if the learners have been appropriately supported for skill and knowledge development, and that support has led to a high overall success rate for the programme.

| Inspection organizations | Inspection organizations such as Ofsted for England, The Education and Training Inspectorate for Northern Ireland, Estyn for Wales or Education Scotland will provide wide-ranging feedback about the success of the whole organization. Not only will they consider the overall success rates of individual programmes, they will also make judgements about retention and attendance of learners. All of which will provide confirmation about the quality of the learning programme. They will also review, amongst other things, the impact of the learner journey in reaching the learning outcomes, health and safety and how the programme has met the needs and interests of learners. Importantly, inspectors will review the way leaders and managers promote and manage a positive learning culture. |

Web box

It is useful to know the criteria for the judgements that are made about the effectiveness of teaching, learning and assessment by the inspection bodies. You can download the inspection frameworks from:

Nation	Organization	Web address
Wales	Estyn	http://www.estyn.gov.uk/
Northern Ireland	Education and Training Inspectorate	http://www.etini.gov.uk/
Scotland	Education Scotland	http://www.educationscotland.gov.uk/
England	Ofsted	http://www.ofsted.gov.uk/

Completing a scheme of work

There are no set rules about how the scheme of work should look and there are as many templates for schemes of work as there are learning providers. You may be in a position where you have to design your own scheme of work. Or the format is sometimes predetermined, in which case all curriculum areas within the same organization will be required to use the same template. However, all schemes of work, even if they are on the same template, will differ. Each will be for a different subject or topic and based on some or all of the six questions above. And, as they are used, each one will be individualized as they become the working and evaluative document of the teacher leading the programme.

Online reference document

You can download a template for a scheme of work from *the Effective Teaching and Learning resource website: Chapter 3*.

Lesson planning

Adopting a cycle of continuous development for the individual learning sessions helps to ensure that teaching and learning are safe, enjoyable and effective in meeting the needs and interests of learners.

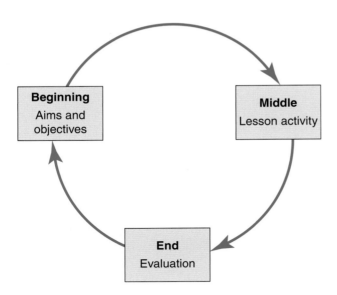

The lesson plan

If the scheme of work is well designed, the lesson plan will 'fall out' of the curriculum plan. A good lesson plan will be structured, yet flexible. It will have a beginning, middle and end. The lesson plan will allow you to 'rehearse' the teaching and learning session you are going to deliver. By planning each activity, you will have the opportunity to run through how they might work before using them in the learning session. It will be designed to meet the needs of all learners and will be developed using information about learners gathered from a wide range of sources collated over a period of time. This type of information is sometimes known as 'initial assessment'.

Important note

The best initial assessment *is actually* ongoing assessment. *Each time a learner completes a learning session and a form of assessment is carried out, new and emerging information which will further support learning will be identified. This ongoing assessment of individual learner needs will help to identify the support that is required for the learner to succeed.*

Initial and ongoing assessment may include information about:

- Previous or existing learning or experience related to the subject content.
- The level at which the learner functions for literacy and numeracy.
- The preferred learning style of the learner.
- The psychometric or psychological measurement of the learner.
- The external support that the learner may (or may not) have – for example, through school, employers, parents, carers, home or working life.
- Any barriers to learning that may be present, such as additional physical, personal, learning or social needs, and sometimes in the case of hairdressing learners, dyslexia.
- Identification of areas of difficulty of knowledge and/or skills.

Components of a lesson plan

The template for lesson plans will vary, but as a minimum a good lesson plan template will include the following:

1 The beginning

- Aims for the lesson
- Objectives of the lesson

2 The middle

- Identification of the specific needs of learners
- Reference to employer support and training that may be provided and will complement the lesson
- Reference to the integrated aspects that are embedded within the curriculum and delivered in lessons, such as:
  - literacy and numeracy skills
  - equality and diversity
  - health and safety
  - safeguarding
  - themes of every child matters

- Teaching and learning strategies and methods that will be used
- Assessment methods that will be used, such as:
  - assessment *for* learning
  - assessment *of* learning
- Differentiated activities to ensure there is sufficient support as well as 'stretch and challenge' for all learners

3 The end

- Evaluation of the lesson

1 The beginning (aims and objectives)

Effective lesson planning includes using clear aims and measurable objectives. These will enable differentiated learning through appropriate teaching and learning activities, which will support successful learning. With successful learning, overall success rates are more likely to be increased. This may sound easy but planning for teaching and learning is like any skill, it needs to be practised.

The beginning of the lesson delivery starts with the completion of the aims and objectives. It is important to clearly identify the differences between 'aims' and 'objectives'.

Aims The aims should provide the overall context for the lesson. They are likely to be quite general, can be descriptive and are often written from a teacher, rather than a learner, perspective. They are not entirely measurable, nor are they intended to be. The aim will provide an overview of what is going to be covered and may include the stage of the learning journey the lesson has been developed for. For example, the teacher might state that the planned lesson is one of five on a given subject. This provides the current context for the session and demonstrates a sound and ongoing framework for the *learning objectives*. It may state the level of the learners or the point at which they are in their overall learning programme.

Example aim

Introduction of basic hair cutting techniques to first year apprentices. In this first session of four, following a demonstration, apprentices will practise the one length haircut on blocks or live models using a range of different tools and equipment following appropriate health and safety requirements.

Objectives Unlike aims, objectives are measurable. It is because they are measurable that teachers and learners will be able to accurately measure the extent to which the learning objectives have been met. Good learning objectives are also learner-centred and shared with learners at the beginning, throughout and at the end of the lesson.

For individualized learning, it is important to have learning objectives that all learners in the group can achieve. Therefore, several different levels of learning objectives may need to be written. Learning outcomes are measured in a variety of ways, which can include observation, verbal confirmation or some form of formal or informal assessment.

However, objectives cannot be measured unless they have been written in a form which uses measurable language. Measurable learning objectives are written using a verb at the beginning of the statement. The verb may be related to the development or mastery of a skill or of knowledge. The language used to write the learning objective should be such that by the end of the teaching and learning session, both the teacher and the learner can clearly state the extent to which the learning objective has been met.

FOR EXAMPLE

At the end of the lesson:

All learners will be able to:

- Meet all health and safety requirements for cutting hair.
- Describe the purpose of the tools and equipment required for carrying out a one length hair cut.
- Use the correct tools and equipment for a one length hair cut.
- Control hair by sectioning correctly for a one length hair cut.
- Carry out a one length hair cut on a block or live model with teacher support.
- Evaluate their own performance.

Some learners will be able to:

- Manage and independently complete a one length hair cut on a block or live model.
- Judge the accuracy of their own cutting skills.

The language used for the learning objectives on page 65 will enable the teacher and the learner to evaluate the extent to which the learning objective has been met. This is because they are SMART.

The objectives are **Specific**	They clearly state what the learner should be able to do and how they are to do it.
The objectives are **Measurable**	The verb that fronts the learning objective allows the teacher to confirm the extent to which the objectives were met (or not). For example, all health and safety requirements were met. Or, if they were not fully met, the teacher and learner will be able to identify which were met. The learner could describe (or not) the purpose of the tools and equipment to be used and the correct tools were used (or not) etc.

The objectives are **achievable**	By all or some of the learners. The objectives indicate that some learners may be able to complete their work independently, without teacher support.
The objectives are **realistic**	They are learner-centred and they build on simple to more complex skills.
The objectives are **time bound**	The learning outcomes will be completed by the end of the lesson.

RESEARCH ACTIVITY

On page 57 in this chapter there is a research activity to investigate Bloom's Taxonomy. Apply Bloom's Taxonomy to the learning objectives listed in the example above. Note how the simpler tasks lead to more complex skills. Then apply the principles to your own lesson plans to confirm the skills and knowledge included build in a coherent way.

Online reference document

You can download examples of verbs that can be used to write learning outcomes or to plan questions. The verbs are categorized, for ease of use, into different types of learning related to Bloom's Taxonomies of cognitive, psychomotor and affective domains. The subdivisions of the different categories allow you to develop knowledge, skills and attitudes from simple to the most complex.

2 The middle (lesson delivery)

The middle aspect lesson planning refers to aspects of delivery such as:

a. How learning supports the specific needs of learners.
b. How learning links to and complements that provided by employers.
c. How learning is linked to safeguarding, equality and diversity, health and safety, themes of every child matters and literacy and numeracy skills.

d. The teaching and learning strategies and methods that will be used.
e. The methods of assessment that will be used.
f. How differentiated opportunities for meeting the individual needs of learners will be met.

a) Supporting the specific needs of learners It is important to remove any barriers that may impede learning. There are many reasons why learners will have a barrier for learning.

Barriers to learning may include:

- *Additional learning needs* – support may be required for literacy and numeracy skills or for information technology. Learners may have dyslexia, dyspraxia or dyscalculia.

- *Additional social needs* – support may be required for learners who may be unemployed, with family problems, are carers or single parents, or are without a permanent home.

- *Additional psychological needs* – support may be required for emotional or behavioural issues which distract learners from learning. Some learners may be very introverted and as such are less likely to ask for additional support and guidance. Conversely, some learners who display more extrovert behaviour may also need additional support to allow them to concentrate and focus on the work required for successful learning outcomes.

- *Additional physical needs* – support may be required for learners who may have long-term, or persistent and frequent short-term illness. Some learners may have sensory impairments such as eyesight or hearing and need support for these aspects. Some conditions may be an indication that the learner is predisposed to allergies, for example, eczema and asthma. This may impact when using the chemicals required for services in hairdressing and thus would be a barrier for learning.

Effective initial and ongoing assessment will help you to identify individual needs of learners; and identify ways to lift barriers so all can achieve at a level that is appropriate for them.

b) How learning links to and complements that provided by employers While it is important to recognize that some learners complete vocational programmes for self-fulfilment purposes, for most, the primary purpose of vocational learning is to gain employment within the hairdressing industry. For this reason, employer engagement is a vital tool for the development of learning programmes and lesson delivery. You have to be sure that the curriculum you are delivering will equip learners for employment at an appropriate level.

Wherever you have learners that are employed, effective initial and ongoing assessment will help to identify the type, frequency and level of training that takes place in the workplace, or *'on the job'*. The *'off the job'* curriculum, the aspect delivered by a learning provider, should complement and support that provided by the employer.

Where learners are not currently employed, it is still important to link the delivery of your curriculum to the needs of employers. Working in partnership with employers helps to ensure that local training needs and labour demands are met.

RESEARCH ACTIVITY

Re-look at your curriculum offer with colleagues. How does your curriculum link with the needs of your local and national employers?

c) How learning is linked to safeguarding, equality and diversity, health and safety, themes of every child matters and skills for literacy and numeracy

For some learning programmes, the full curriculum content may include more than just the main *learning aims*. For example, along with the delivery of the main qualification, there is also a requirement to embed or enhance topics that can be integrated during lesson delivery.

These may include:

- Safeguarding
- Equality and diversity
- Health and safety
- Themes of every child matters
- Literacy and numeracy skills
- Personal, learning and thinking skills

There are always opportunities to embed and integrate such topics through the naturally occurring evidence of the main qualification. Indeed, in many cases, with the thorough and effective embedding of such subjects, learners are more able to see the direct correlation of the topics and apply skills and knowledge in a hairdressing-related task.

Online reference document

You can download a document *Integrating Additional Topics*, from *the Effective Teaching and Learning resource website: Chapter 3* which provides guidance of how health and safety, equality and diversity, and safeguarding can be integrated and embedded with the delivery of hairdressing programmes using naturally occurring opportunities.

Important note

It is really vital to note that no matter how well peripheral topics are planned, embedded or integrated, unless you as the teacher highlight and emphasize them, learners will fail to recognize their importance, link them to their everyday activities or recognize that they have applied the skills.

d) The teaching and learning strategies and methods that will be used In Chapter 4 you will find information about teaching and learning strategies and methods. The chapter highlights the importance of adopting the correct strategy to deliver appropriate teaching and learning methods that meet the individual needs and interests of your learners. The key to an engaging learning experience is to focus lesson delivery on active, learner participation through a variety of well planned and meaningful tasks.

e) The methods of assessment that will be used In Chapter 5 you will find information about different assessment methods. The chapter outlines the importance of assessment *for* learning as a tool for evaluation and action planning future teaching and learning sessions. In addition, the conditions for meeting the awarding body requirements for assessment *of* learning are outlined.

f) How differentiated opportunities for meeting the individual needs for learners will be met When planning your lesson, you must be able to ensure that the needs of all learners are met. Not all learners learn at the same time, you may have a wide range of learning needs within the same learning group. Some learners may learn quickly, and if such learners are not sufficiently challenged, they may lose interest and could potentially leave the programme. Others may learn more slowly, or the pace of the lesson may be too brisk. This again will be disengaging, learners will lose interest and they too could potentially leave the programme.

It is not easy to meet a wide variety of learning needs, but with good planning, successful learning outcomes are more likely to be achieved by all. There are, however, a range of strategies that can be used to support differentiated or individualized learning.

- **Have clear and accurate information about the learning characteristics of your group.** Utilize the initial and ongoing assessment collated at the beginning and throughout the learning programmes to develop learner-centred, active learning activities which support the preferred learning styles of individuals within the group. You can find out more about initial assessment in Chapter 5 Assessment.

- **Plan learning using a multi-sensory approach to teaching and learning methods**. Learners with dyslexia benefit from a multi-sensory approach to teaching and learning. Adopting this approach will mean that all other learners will benefit. You can read more about this is Chapter 2 on page 44.

- **Have a logical approach to the development of skills and knowledge.** All learners, regardless of their ability, learn best if new topics are introduced by first developing the simplest aspects of skills, attitudes or knowledge before moving on to the more complex development of skills, attitudes or knowledge.

- **Adapt the time for the learning task.** Learners complete tasks at different rates and it is important to maintain interest and motivation for those who work quickly. On completion of the main task have a linked, ready prepared extension activity that will develop further learning skills. For those who may take longer, consider giving information to learners prior to the learning session so they can prepare for the task.

- **Simplify or amplify the task.** When developing tasks to meet the learning objectives, be prepared to simplify or amplify the task to meet individual needs. Simplify the task for learners who need further support and guidance by breaking the task down into smaller, more achievable steps. Conversely, for those who learn quickly, amplify the task to increase the level of difficulty, or breadth of learning to further challenge and motivate learners.

- **Use the strengths of peers.** Exploit the talents of individuals within the group and pair up or create teams of learners using their individual strengths to ensure peer support and self-development skills of mentoring.

- *Maximize the opportunities of assessment for learning.*
  Don't wait until the end of a teaching and learning session to carry out an evaluation. Use assessment *for* learning as a tool to assess where learners are, at critically strategic points throughout the lesson. Then, move the lesson forward at an appropriate level and pace based on the evaluation of each assessment *for* learning technique you use. By doing so, you can adapt your lesson plan to provide more support or increase the challenge for those who need it. You will learn more about assessment *for* learning in Chapter 5.

And, if you are able:

- *Provide individual, one-to-one support for learners.*
  Individual or one-to-one teaching and learning support provided by a teaching assistant is invaluable, but is not always available for all. If you have a learning support assistant, then the lesson plan should include how this level of support will be utilized in the teaching and learning session. Effective planning can ensure that the impact of such specialized support can benefit the learning experience for all learners in the group. Individual support is as beneficial for learners who excel in their work as it is for those who require support to progress.

3 The end (evaluation)

It is only through good and effective evaluation that teachers and learners are able to assess the extent to which the learning outcomes have been met. The best evaluations are learner-centred. This means the learner can tell the teacher what they have learned, not the other way around, where the teacher tells the learners what they have learned. Armed with this information, the teacher can accurately plan and prepare for the next teaching and learning session providing the support identified through evaluation.

In Chapter 4 you will find information about a range of activities that can be used to effectively evaluate your lessons.

Online reference document

You can download a template for a lesson plan from *the Effective Teaching and Learning resource website: Chapter 3*. An example lesson is provided for reference.

Development checklist

Visit *the Effective Teaching and Learning resource website* to download a development checklist summarizing what you have covered in Chapter 3.

CHAPTER 4

Teaching and learning strategies and methods

Tell me and I forget, teach me and I may remember, involve me and I learn.

Benjamin Franklin 1706–1790 American Politician and Author

INTRODUCTION

This chapter summarizes teaching and learning methodologies. Choosing the most appropriate strategies and methods for teaching and learning is vital if you want to ensure that the needs and interests of learners are met and that learners are actively involved in their learning. To engage learners, learning needs to be motivating, interesting and inspiring. It takes time to develop effective teaching and learning techniques. However, with time comes practise and like any skill, practise makes perfect. To keep the learning experience fresh, new and engaging, you can, over a period, begin to introduce some new teaching and learning strategies and methods. One way of looking at a good learning experience is to link learning to as many senses as possible, making learning multi-sensory. By including an assortment of learning techniques you can provide variety and an element of planned surprise to enhance the learners' experience. To do this, as with an appetizing and satisfying meal, you need a 'menu' of activities to choose from. The chapter will explore teaching methods that can be used for starters (warm up activities), the main course (the delivery of the main teaching and learning outcomes) and dessert (plenary and evaluation activities). A very, enticing, learning meal….

CHAPTER LEARNING OBJECTIVES

This chapter will support the development of:

....

- Identification and application of a range of teaching and learning strategies, methods and activities
- Creation of a teaching and learning portfolio
- Differentiated teaching and learning

Teaching and learning strategies and methods

It is difficult to pinpoint an absolutely clear, definitive definition of the differences between teaching and learning *strategies* and teaching and learning *methods*, with the terms frequently interchanged. The following definition has been developed to support a clearer distinction between the two terms, and, from experience has proved to be useful with teachers struggling to understand the concepts.

In simple terms the teaching *strategy* is the overarching, planned framework for the delivery of a teaching and learning session. The teaching *method* is the vehicle or tools you will use during the session to achieve the learning outcomes.

Teaching strategies

The *teaching strategy* is based on the number and interaction of learners and teachers within a given environment.

You need to know:

- The numbers of learners in the group you will be teaching.
- The numbers of teachers that will be supporting the learning experience.
- The environment in which you will be teaching.

For example, in order to effectively plan your session using appropriate teaching methods, you need to know the number of learners in the group. The options you have for teaching and learning methods with very small numbers of learners may vary from those for large groups.

You also need to know how many teachers will be available during the session. For example, you may be, or have the support of, a support teacher or a colleague for team teaching. Typically in hairdressing, you may be working in a team with a technician who will be able to provide technical support for learners. Each person needs to have a defined role – and this is part of your strategy.

In addition the environment must be considered. To deliver a practical hairdressing session, you need access to a suitable learning environment, for example, in a realistic learning or working environment. If you are delivering a theory session, a classroom with tables and chairs is likely to be the most appropriate learning environment.

Therefore, the teaching *strategy* for hairdressing subjects will include learners and teachers working and/or interacting:

- Individually
- In pairs
- In groups
- In teams

With learning being facilitated by:

- A single teacher
- Two or more teachers (team teaching)
- A teacher and support assistant(s)
- A teacher and support technician for technical work
- A teacher and outside experts such as those representing hairdressing manufacturers
- A combination of any of the above

With the session topic delivered in a learning environment such as a:

- Commercial hairdressing salon
- Training salon – realistic working environment (RWE) or realistic learning environment (RLE)

- Classroom
- Science laboratory
- Library
- Resource centre
- ICT suite
- Virtual learning environment

For example, in Chapter 2 you will find a downloadable example of a lesson plan. Within the plan you will see the strategy defined as:

Teaching and learning strategies: *Group, individual and pair work carried out in realistic working environment hairdressing salon with support of teaching assistant.*

Teaching and learning methods

While teaching and learning *strategies* are your 'framework' and relate to the number of learners and teachers, how they will interact and the environment they will work in, teaching and learning *methods* are your 'tools' and should be appropriate for the job you wish to do. This means the methods must be suitable for the individual needs and characteristics of your learners and for the desired learning outcomes.

> **Important note**
>
> *The chosen teaching and learning method should be used to stimulate, challenge and inform learning. In good or better sessions, teaching methods are typically varied and delivered at a pace to maintain the interest of all learners.*

For example, in Chapters 2 and 3 you will find downloadable examples of a lesson plan. Within the plan you will see the variety of methods defined as:

Teaching and learning methods: *Demonstration, demonstration/ discussion intervention (Equality, Diversity and Inclusion (EDI), safeguarding, health and safety, literacy and numeracy skills, Every Child Matters (ECM), Personal Learning and Thinking Skills (PLTS)) individual skill development through peer support, modelling and experiential learning.*

Research, in particular that led by Professor John Hattie, shows that learners learn best when they are directly involved in their own learning. This contrasts with the view that learners are passive and that the teacher alone, solely holds responsibility for imparting knowledge and skills. However this does not mean that a class-centred approach is never used. You should use a range of methods to meet the needs and interests of your learners, including:

- ***Learner-centred activities*** – where learners learn at their own pace and may be engaged in different levels of the same activities in the same learning session. For example, all learners may be practising a particular hairdressing skill, but some will progress more quickly than others.

- ***Whole class-centred sessions*** – where all learners learn the same subject at the same time in the same learning session. For example, when introducing a brand new hairdressing theory or concept in which none of the learners will have any prior knowledge or experience.

- ***Resource-centred learning*** – where learners use a range of resources such as electronic learning, work books and interactive teaching resources to learn the same things at different times, sometimes in their own time, but can be in the same session. For example, during the completion of projects and assignments or with research activities associated with the hairdressing programme.

Web box

A good, interesting and short summary on Hattie's research and what has the greatest influence on learning can be found here: http://www.teacherstoolbox.co.uk/T_effect_sizes.html.

 RESEARCH ACTIVITY

Look at the chart devised by Professor Hattie and see if you already use any of the learning methods listed. Check out the 'effect size' on learning. Are you using the methods that have the greatest effect on learning?

For active, learner-centred learning to be successful; teachers must prepare learners to take on some responsibility for their own learning.

Important note

Remember that there has to be a beginning, middle and an end for each learning session. And, because you need to use the results of learners' learning outcomes for future planning at the end of the session, you will find there will always be a new beginning for the next session based on the individual requirements of learners.

Preparing learners for learner-centred learning

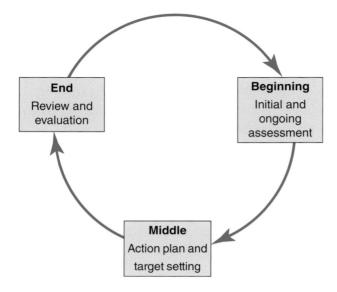

Beginning Work with the learners and use information gathered through initial and ongoing assessment to identify current and existing skills and knowledge. Then, develop a personalized learning programme. The individualized programme will link into your lesson plan. Within the lesson plan you will be able to highlight the specific support a learner may require to achieve their learning outcomes.

Middle Work with the learner to develop an action plan. Identify any support that needs to be in place to ensure a successful outcome for the learning session or programme and set negotiated and achievable targets for each stage of the learning programme. Some of the teaching and learning methods you use will be derived from the outcomes of the assessment for learning you have completed with learners.

End Regularly review and evaluate the effectiveness of support and meeting of the learners' targets. Identify current skills and knowledge using assessment for learning techniques. Refer to the results of ongoing assessment to identify new areas of support and set new, negotiated and achievable targets through effective action planning. Use the information to inform the *Individual Learning Plan* (ILP).

Important note

You will find more information about planning for the beginning, the middle and the end of learning sessions in Chapter 3 on page 61.

Applying different teaching methods

Choosing the right teaching and learning method depends on the influences that will be included in your strategy, such as the interaction of learners and teachers in the given environment, as well as the learning outcomes. Your teaching and learning methods are your tools. You need to choose an appropriate tool to enable learners to achieve the learning outcomes.

You need to know:

- The aims and objectives for the session.
- How long the session will last – so the appropriate number of tasks can be included.
- The characteristics of the learners – to support individualized and differentiated learning.
- The preferred learning styles of learners.
- The results of initial and ongoing assessment for individual learners – to support individualized and differentiated learning.
- The outcomes of assessment for learning – so teaching methods can be adapted to suit the needs of learners.
- How you are going to assess the learning.

And importantly:

- Methods that you are comfortable to use.

Overarching teaching and learning methods

There are many different teaching and learning methods for you to choose from. Using the definition that teaching and learning *methods* are the 'tools' used to deliver the learning outcomes there are some overarching methods from which different teaching and learning activities can be developed. Examples of overarching teaching and learning methods include the following recognized approaches for effective teaching and learning[1]:

- Cooperative learning
- Experiential learning
- Relating theory and practice
- Multi-sensory learning
- Modelling
- Learning conversations
- e-learning and technology

---

[1] Source: Effective teaching and learning Excellence Gateway – 10 pedagogy approaches

Web box

You can find out more about the approaches to teaching and learning that have been included in this chapter from: http://tlp.excellencegateway.org.uk/tlp/ pedagogy/introducingthe1/introducingthe1/index.html.

Using the underlying principles from each of these overarching methods you can develop a range of teaching and learning activities that is only limited by your own imagination.

For example, by using the principles of cooperative learning, which encourages team work across groups of learners that may not naturally work together, you can develop activities such as 'jigsaw' and 'numbered heads together'. By using experiential learning you can develop a wide range of activities in which learners are required to implement the underlying principles of do, reflect, analyze and apply.

Using cooperative learning

This is a powerful teaching and learning method which enables individuals to work together in small teams with a variety of peers to achieve a common aim. It can bring together teams of learners that may not normally work together. Team work is encouraged across racial, gender, age, cultural and social boundaries and backgrounds. In addition, learners of different learning abilities can work together for mutual support and self-development.

By using cooperative learning, all learners can see that they are all as important as each other. And that the success and achievement of the task relies on each and every member of the team effectively working together.

Important note

Unlike other types of group work, with cooperative learning there is no hiding place for those who like to sit back and let others in the group do work for them. Everyone in the group has an element of the task to complete, and unless each member completes their task, all will fail.

RESEARCH ACTIVITY

Dr Spencer Kagan developed the concept of 'Structures'. Structures is a framework for a cooperative learning activity which is not dependent on any particular subject or curriculum content. By using the framework and adding your own curriculum content, you have a cooperative learning activity. You can read more about the research here: http://www.kaganonline.com

Online reference document

Some session activities which incorporate Kagan Structures and cooperative learning include:

- Jigsaw
- Think, Pair and Share
- Team, Pair, Solo
- Numbered heads together

You can download cooperative learning resources based on the teaching and learning methods outlined above from *the Effective Teaching and Learning resource website: Chapter 4.*

Using experiential learning

Experiential learning is learning by experience. This type of learning allows learners to acquire new skills by doing things, and to learn from their mistakes. To be successful, learners also need skills to be able to self-evaluate their experience or performance and to draw critical conclusions that will enable them to apply new, improved learning. The method engages learners in real, first hand experience which allows them to learn as they are making discoveries. Learners are able to construct meaning and develop understanding from their learning experience.

The key to experiential learning is the opportunity to reflect on learning. Reflection allows learners to identify what they have done well, and what they might do better next time. Following reflection, the learner applies readjusted skills and knowledge and once again, reflects on their learning experience again, identifying what they have done well and what they might improve next time.

Important note

This learning method needs to be used carefully. While learners benefit from identifying how they can improve by learning from their mistakes, for some, making mistakes can be discouraging and demotivating. To prevent negativity when using this method, use the learners' initial and ongoing assessment results to devise individualized activities that are challenging, yet achievable. Results of the assessment and learning outcomes should be noted during the evaluation of the learning session, so appropriate planning and support can be provided in future sessions. Even better, ask learners to keep a reflective log so they can clearly see the progress they are making.

Without realizing it, most practical hairdressing learning is actually based on this learning method. All hairdressing skills are practised over a period of time, reviewed, analyzed and improvements are identified – consciously or subconsciously before using the identified improvements to further improve skills.

In Chapter 2 you can read about the experiential learning cycle developed by David Kolb on pages 40–41.

Online reference document

Some session activities which incorporate experiential learning can be downloaded from *the Effective Teaching and Learning resource website: Chapter 4.*

Using relating theory to practice and practice to theory

This is another 'tool' that can be used for effective teaching and learning and can be combined with experiential learning. When relating practice to theory, learning is active and learner-centred. However, when relating theory to practice, the teacher leads by providing or facilitating the learner with the existing theory. In both cases learners are engaged in the learning cycle, either moving from an abstract concept to concrete concept or from concrete concepts to abstract. This particular teaching and learning is flexible in that the two approaches can be combined to a cycle of theory to practice and back to theory, or vice versa.

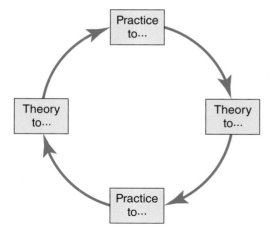

Practice to theory (moving from the concrete to abstract)

This teaching and learning method enables a learner-led approach to problem solving. Learning begins with the problem. This could be, for example, a case study. Learners solve the problem using a range of different learning techniques. This learning can be facilitated through independent research, by discussing the problem with peers or through experimenting with different concepts. One critical aspect of this method is that once learners have determined their answers to the problem, the final proof of their accuracy is that the answers should work in any other identical situation. A benefit of using this technique is that learners acquire a deeper understanding of the theories related to the task.

Relating practice to theory

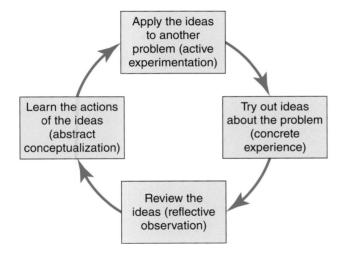

Theory to practice (moving from abstract to concrete)

This method begins with a teacher-led approach. The teacher provides, or facilitates, learning of the theory. Then learners apply the given theory in a practical situation. There are some aspects of hairdressing that, for health and safety reasons, learners need to clearly understand the theory of before they can begin to apply their knowledge in a practical way. A good example of this is colouring hair. To prevent damage to hair and skin, learners need to understand the theoretic concepts of the international colour chart, of depth and tone as well as the properties of colour products and activators before they can apply such knowledge to using colours.

Relating theory to practice

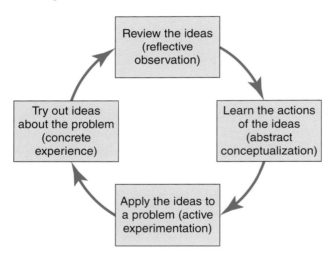

RESEARCH ACTIVITY

Relating theory to practice or vice versa involves two quite different approaches to learning. The approaches are *deductive reasoning* and *inductive reasoning*. Investigate the principles that underpin these approaches, see how they link with relating theory and practice and apply the concepts in your own teaching and learning.

Web box

....

A useful article by QIA on problem solving and pedagogy: http://tlp.excellence gateway.org.uk/tlp/cpd/assets/documents/it_problem_solving_approaches.rtf.

Online reference document

Some example activities which incorporate relating theory and practice can be downloaded from *the Effective Teaching and Learning resource website: Chapter 4.*

Using multi-sensory learning

This is highly recommended for effective teaching and learning. One of the main benefits of this method of teaching and learning is that it incorporates the senses of touch, sight, hearing and sometimes smell, and for some subjects, taste, which means that the preferred learning styles are accommodated. Thus, the learning experience is enriched for all:

- The sense of sight is linked to the learning style preferred by visual learners.
- The sense of hearing is linked to the preferred learning style of auditory learners.
- The sense of touch and smell is linked to the preferred learning style of kinaesthetic learners.

You can find more information about learning styles in Chapter 2 on pages 37–38.

Important note

While it is useful to identify a preferred learning style which can be used as a starting point for lesson planning, the best learning occurs when a variety of learning styles are used. By doing so, a multi-sensory approach to teaching and learning can be developed.

The best learning occurs when all senses are engaged, as by doing this the learner is able to create more 'constructs', making learning more memorable. Combining all three senses with, in the case of hairdressing, the occasional addition of smell, provides the perfect ingredients for a multi-sensory learning experience.

Some examples to:

Enhance the visual aspects of your multi-sensory session

- Create mood boards to reinforce the visual perspective of your topic.
- Show real, finished or step by step examples of the learning outcomes.
- Show the end result – let learners know what they are aiming for.
- Show relevant and up to date DVDs to support the skill learners are practising.
- Colour code instructions for learners to follow, perhaps highlighting those that might link to health and safety, equality and diversity or literacy and numeracy in different, but consistent colours.
- Use mind mapping to explain processes – either paper-based or using relevant software.
- Display colourful key words and posters on walls to support continuous subliminal learning.

Enhance the auditory aspects of your multi-sensory session

- Encourage active and meaningful discussions between learners.
- Create raps, rhymes and musical reminders about the key facts learners have to remember.
- Maximize peer support, such as using peers to explain or repeat key concepts.
- Record and download information onto personal MP3s.
- Ask learners to repeat key phrases out loud to make the sounds memorable.

Enhance the kinesthetic aspects of your multi-sensory session

....

- Encourage learners to move around during theory sessions instead of remaining seated in the same place.
- Take learners into different environments to support learning – VLEs, libraries, science laboratories, salons, workshops.
- Allow learners to touch and handle resources and products when first introducing them, and if it is safe to do so, to feel and smell them too.
- Give learners time to practise different sequences to reinforce the movements they make for different practical tasks.
- Use role play to support learning for communication, client care and consultation techniques.

Online reference document

Example activities based on multi-sensory learning can be downloaded from *the Effective Teaching and Learning resource website: Chapter 4.* The activities include case studies for colouring, cutting or plaiting hair. Within each example are directions of how you can use the activities to accommodate visual, auditory, reading/writing and kinaesthetic learning styles.

Web box

A short but interesting paper relating to multi-sensory learning can be found on
the Excellence Gateway website: http://tlp.excellencegateway.org.uk/tlp/
pedagogy/assets/documents/qs_multi_sensory_learning.pdf.

Using modelling

This teaching and learning method relies on experts to model a skill or
process. American educational psychologists, Paul Eggen and Don
Kauchak, describe modelling as *'changes in people that result from
observing the actions of others.'* The changes learners make can be
related to a range of different aspects. For example, their competencies
and creativity, in how they communicate, how they speak and write.
Or, modelling can be related to attitudes and values.

> **Important note**
>
> *The key concept about modelling is that learners see how an expert makes, says or does
> something and then replicates what they have witnessed, seen or heard.*

Modelling promotes positive role models. Opportunities for modelling
can be developed using a range of experts. For example, apart from
teachers, learners could model from visiting speakers, hairdressing
manufacturers' technicians, hairdressing employers and, importantly,
from peers. Learning developed from peers is a powerful concept and
memorable, sometimes more so than that from their teacher.

When using modelling, walk the learner through your mind – tell them
what you are doing, what you are feeling, what you see and hear.
Break tasks into small bite-sized pieces. Allow learners to master each
piece of the whole. Adapt the detail you use in your modelling to
balance with the amount of experience and expertise they already
have. Learners brand new to tasks will require a deeper explanation
than those who have previous experience. Support modelling with
experiential learning to reinforce learning and to allow learners to

reflect on their achievements, recognize what they have learned, and then implement the improvements they have identified.

It is important to share learning outcomes with learners. One way of doing this, in relation to modelling, is to show finished examples of the learning objective. You might show assignments that have been completed to a range of different standards. You might also demonstrate a particular hairdressing technique or client care routine for learners to copy.

Important note

In relation to the practical skills, there is also a disadvantage to modelling. Hairdressing is a very creative skill and the learner's own, individual and imaginative techniques should be nurtured and developed. Therefore, modelling should be used carefully to reinforce exemplar work without the expectation of learners becoming clones of the experts.

Modelling can also work in reverse. For example, when setting a new assignment for learners, complete the assignment yourself in 'real time'. By doing yourself what you are expecting your learners to do, will highlight the problems they may encounter. Perhaps the information they need to research is too difficult to locate, the assignment may be too long or the length of time allowed too demanding. Conversely, you may find that the assignment provides too little interest to motivate and inspire, or is too easy and will not stretch and challenge your learners. At the end of your 'real time' work, you can share your results with your learners as an example from which they can model.

Online reference document

Example activities based on modelling can be downloaded from *the Effective Teaching and Learning resource website: Chapter 4.*

 RESEARCH ACTIVITY

....

A short but interesting paper relating to modelling can be found on the Excellence Gateway website: http://tlp.excellencegateway.org.uk/tlp/pedagogy/assets/documents/qs_modelling.pdf

Using learning conversations

Learning conversations are central to all good one-to-one learning experiences. They are a powerful means of dialogue between the learner and teacher. Learning conversations provide a learner-centred approach to identify support for moving towards their targets and to plan future learning. The teacher skills required for learning conversations rely on the use of good and effective questioning techniques, as well as the ability to listen carefully while learners explain their understanding of learning outcomes and make their concerns, plans and expectations explicit through this conversational approach.

In addition to one-to-one reviews and target setting, learning conversations can also be utilized during session time as assessment for learning. Some of the assessment for learning techniques, which are outlined in Chapter 5, can be extended and the feedback used to develop the learning conversation. For example, learners can use the commonly applied and very effective technique of RAG (red, amber, green) cards as an indicator for their level of understanding. The learning conversation can begin at the point the learner is indicating. By displaying red, the learner is indicating there are barriers to learning. This indicator will instigate a different learning conversation than that for a learner displaying amber or green cards.

Important note

During a learning conversation the teacher will listen to the details that determine how much of the task or topic the learner understands, and use this information to provide challenging methods of improvement.

A key concept of learning conversations is that the conversation does not have to be with the teacher. Peer to peer learning conversations can be very effective and provide a mutually beneficial opportunity for reflection. The reflection aspect can be likened to the experiential learning cycle in that the learner will think about, and then verbally articulate what they would like to achieve, the progress they are making, the skills they have and how they can make improvements and transfer their skill to other situations.

The following learning conversation outline can be applied to hairdressing learners and is contextually adapted from The Institute of Education, University of London, Diana Laurillard's approach to learning conversations:

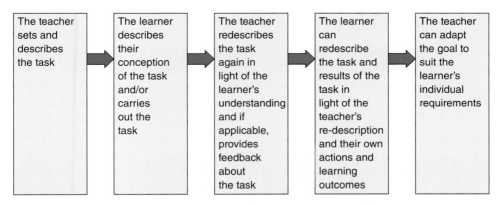

| The teacher sets and describes the task | The learner describes their conception of the task and/or carries out the task | The teacher redescribes the task again in light of the learner's understanding and if applicable, provides feedback about the task | The learner can redescribe the task and results of the task in light of the teacher's re-description and their own actions and learning outcomes | The teacher can adapt the goal to suit the learner's individual requirements |

Source: Atherton J S (2011) *Learning and Teaching; Conversational learning theory; G Pask and D Laurillard*

During the learning conversation, as the learner is learning, the teacher and the learner are engaged in a conversation in which each is sharing their own view about the task. The approach to questioning is critical for effective learning conversations. Questions should be open and teachers should be empathetic, 'standing in the shoes' of the learner. They need to recognize how the learner is feeling. Body language must be non-threatening, and both teachers and learners require good listening skills. Increasing the wait time you have following a question will allow the learners time to reflect and to formulate their responses.

Web box

....

For more on conversation theory visit: http://www.instructionaldesign.org/theories/conversation-theory.html.

Web box

....

A short but interesting paper relating to learning conversations can be found on the Excellence Gateway website: http://tlp.excellencegateway.org.uk/tlp/pedagogy/assets/documents/qs_learning_conversations.pdf.

Online reference document

A diagrammatic explanation to support the implementation of learning conversations for any aspect of teaching and learning for hairdressing can be downloaded from: *the Effective Teaching and Learning resource website: Chapter 4.*

Using e-learning and technology

There has been a revolution in the use of technology to support teaching and learning. However, it is important that this teaching and learning method is used as an appropriate tool to support development, and not just for the sake of using the technology.

Important note

An example of how e-learning can be blended into a learning session can be seen on the 'teaching and learning menu' on pages 103–106 of this chapter.

A definition from JISC, the UK organization for information and digital technologies for education and research, states that e-learning is:

'Learning facilitated and supported through the use of information and communications technology, e-learning may involve some or all of the following:

- *Desk and laptop computers*
- *Software, including assistive software*
- *Interactive whiteboards*
- *Digital cameras*
- *Mobile and wireless tools, including mobile phones*
- *Electronic communication tools, including email, discussion boards, chat facilities and video conferencing*
- *Virtual learning environments (VLEs)'*

One key aspect of using e-learning and technology as a teaching and learning method is that, like other teaching and learning methods, it must be the most appropriate tool to use for the learning aims and to make learning engaging.

Important note

e-learning does not negate you from the responsibility of setting clear aims and measurable objectives for teaching and learning. Learners still need the structure of a session beginning, middle and end, even when using technology independently. You also need to be aware that some learners will be far more confident that others using technology, so differentiation and extended learning opportunities should be part of your lesson plan.

Not all learning providers and learners will have access to all of the above. But for those that have access to some or all, the motivational advantages are clear:

Technology	Examples	Application for hairdressing topics
Desk and laptop computers Electronic tablets and hand-held devices	Used for a range of activities, word processing, spreadsheet and database development, and development of presentations to name but a few. Used well, computers can add another dimension to teaching and learning. Most young people are acutely aware of and use this type of technology easily. Some learners may need additional support. Laptop computers enable accessible, peripatetic delivery of hairdressing topics. Electronic tablets are highly mobile devices that can be used to show apps as a method of reinforcing learning at workstations or for research.	**Word processing** Reference material for learners to keep at the end of learning sessions **Presentations** Keep notes restricted to bullets to highlight important words and phrases. Link to live websites to reinforce learning **Desk and laptop computers** Learners carry out their own research. Use for peripatetic delivery in hairdressing salons **Tablets and hand-held devices** Use for research or during practical practice sessions to reinforce learning

Technology	Examples	Application for hairdressing topics
Software and online learning	The number of mainstream educational programmes for teaching and learning is enormous. e-learning and online hairdressing packages provide an additional dimension to the learning experience.	Use e-learning and online hairdressing packages to reinforce and support more traditional research tools such as text books and learning packages. Other types of software pertinent for hairdressing are reception and salon management systems used in commercial hairdressing salons. The use of such software can be incorporated into reception topics, or if applicable, to higher level programmes such as level 4.
Interactive whiteboards	Used for a vast range of activities. When used well interactive whiteboards can make learning engaging. Any programme that works on a computer and anything you do on a computer can be done on an interactive whiteboard. Avoid using purely for PowerPoint presentations, which can be as limiting as a paper-based learning sessions. And, in addition, if you don't have an interactive whiteboard,	Use for the delivery of all hairdressing-related topics for theory and practical. Involve learners in the interactivity of this teaching and learning tool. Access appropriate video clips to enhance understanding. Games played using the interactive whiteboard are particularly effective and are great tools for assessment for learning, providing instant feedback.

Technology	Examples	Application for hairdressing topics
	remember you can access and use the same programmes using a projector with your laptop.	
Digital cameras	Digital photography using cameras, smart phones, electronic tablets or mobile phones is a great way for learners to record progress.	Images can be used as evidence in portfolios to illustrate learning development and achievements.
Mobile and wireless tools	Having wireless Internet access will enable learning in salons and classrooms without the need for cabled access.	Peripatetic delivery in learners' own salons is made more effective through this type of technology.
Electronic communication tools	Technology allowing access to learning outside mainstream contact hours.	Educational portals and platforms, peer forums and subject related chat rooms extend learning using a method that engages and interests learners. Increased collaboration between learners is encouraged.
Virtual learning environments (VLEs)	Virtual learning environments provide access to learning wherever the student is – at home, in libraries or in the	This type of learning supports differentiation in that learners have continuous access to all their learning

Technology	Examples	Application for hairdressing topics
	learning environment. Learners have the opportunity to extend, enhance and reinforce learning. Learners and teachers are also able to track their progress, providing further information that can be used to enhance and support learning.	resources at any time and can be used for any hairdressing topic.

Online reference document

A fun, engaging and innovative teaching and learning activity which uses mobile technology and QR codes can be downloaded from: *the Effective Teaching and Learning resource website: Chapter 4*.

Web box

There are lots of tutorials that can be viewed to support the use of interactive whiteboards and other learning technologies and can be found through your search engines. A useful reference paper from JISC can be found here: http://www.jisc.ac.uk/uploaded_documents/Interactivewhiteboards.pdf.

Web box

An online hairdressing learning package to support hairdressing qualifications can be purchased from Habia and Cengage Learning: www.habia.org/u2learn/.

Teaching and learning activities

The overarching teaching and learning methods are your 'tools' and can all be used as a vehicle for teaching and learning *activities*. Again, the key to the most effective teaching and learning activity is using the right activity for the desired learning outcome. The activities you can use are too numerous to count, but can include the following, all of which can be delivered using the overarching teaching and learning methods covered in this chapter:

- Games
  - Quizzes – true/false, multiple choice, worksheets, anagrams, crossword, hangman.
  - Card games and exercises – labelling, comparing statements, matching definitions, dominos, ranking exercises.
  - TV favourite games based on formats such as Blockbusters, Bingo, Who Wants to be a Millionaire, Family Fortunes.
  - Treasure Hunt – paper-based or QR Codes.
- Discussions
  - During small group and paired work.
  - Brainstorming in groups or whole class, importantly, visually noting all contributions and ideas regardless of their relevance or appropriateness (usually writing them on flip charts, white or smart boards).
  - Round robin in which all learners have the opportunity to participate and express their point of view during discussions.
- Role play
  - Paired
  - Group
- Simulations
  - When the 'real' event may never happen – for example, evacuation of a salon.
- Demonstration
- Research

- Presentation
  - To peers
  - To an invited audience
- Practical work
- Experiments
  - To support scientific principles underpinning hairdressing theory.
- Project work
- Visits or visiting speakers
- Case studies

Web box
....
Many of the templates for the TV-based quiz games that can be adapted for teaching and learning can be found using TES Resources. www.tes.co.uk/teaching-resources/.

Web box
....
This site has some ready-made Blockbuster-type games, or you can make your own: http://www.teachers-direct.co.uk/resources/quiz-busters/index.aspx.

A menu for teaching and learning

One way to ensure that learners are motivated and engaged in learning is to vary the teaching and learning methods you use. If you use the same methods for every learning session, your learners will know what to expect before they come to their learning session and they may become complacent. Providing a variety of experiences can be likened to choosing a feast from an enticing menu. In each of your sessions, try to use a teaching and learning method that will support a range of different preferred learning styles. By doing so, even without too much thought you will have the basis for a multi-sensory learning session, which supports learning for all.

For an enticing meal you need to have a 'starter' (to begin the learning process), a 'main course' (to meet the aims and objectives of the learning session) and a 'dessert' (an evaluation activity to check learning).

In the table below is an example of a session related to shampooing and conditioning. The teaching and learning session has the following objectives:

1 Identify a range of shampoos and conditioners used for professional use.
2 Identify relevant questions to ask during a consultation for a shampoo and conditioning treatment.
3 Carry out a shampoo and conditioning consultation and treatment on peers or client.

The session includes moving learners into different environments, but the session could be delivered in RLE or RWE with the use of laptops/electronic tablets and Internet connection. The delivery could be completed offering the following 'menu':

'Menu'	Strategy	Method (including assessment for learning and periodic plenaries throughout all activities)	Activity
'Starter' (recap activity related to previous learning) Activity to recap from previous learning	Individual or paired work in classroom	Multi-sensory	*Game* – *Bingo* recapping on previously learned shampoo and conditioning terminology

'Menu'	Strategy	Method (including assessment for learning and periodic plenaries throughout all activities)	Activity
'Main course' (learning outcomes) 1. Identify a range of shampoos and conditioners used for professional use	Group work in classroom or other environment with Internet access	Cooperative learning e-Learning	*Research* – *Think pair and share.* Stage 1: learners research the different types of products they are aware of. Stage 2: Learners discuss findings in pairs. Stage 3: Pairs share their work with the rest of the group
2. Identify relevant questions to ask during a consultation for a shampoo and conditioning treatment	Paired work in classroom	Theory to practice	*Discussion* – facilitated completion of consultation sheet with key questions to ask clients prior to a shampoo treatment

'Menu'	Strategy	Method (including assessment for learning and periodic plenaries throughout all activities)	Activity
3. Carry out a shampoo and conditioning consultation and treatment on peers or client	Individual or paired work in salon	Modelling and experiential learning	*Practical* – completion of treatment following teacher demonstration
'Dessert' (Plenary and evaluation) Evaluate the quality and effectiveness of the shampoo and conditioning service	Individual and paired work in salon	Experiential learning Learning conversation	*Evaluation* – *Two GHDs and one restyle* activity for self and/or peer evaluation. Plan future learning based on outcomes of evaluation

Web box

....

A useful site for the generation of Bingo cards you can devise from your own word lists and clues can be found here: http://saksena.net/partygames/bingo/.

Web box

....

For a teacher tool box for a range of downloads to support teaching and learning visit: http://www.teacherstoolbox.co.uk/index.html.

Web box

....

For general information about teaching and learning visit: http://www.geoffpetty.com/index.html.

And for more information about online lectures about teaching and learning delivered by Geoff Petty visit: http://www.ifl.ac.uk/cpd/cpd-guidance-and-resources/ask-geoff/geoff.

Embedding differentiated learning

Differentiation is ensuring that the planning for teaching and learning includes strategies and methods that will meet the individual needs of **all** your learners. Remember that it is important to meet the needs and interests of those learners that are very able as well as those who are less so. Learning experiences must be sufficiently and individually challenging for all so that every learner can demonstrate what they know and what they understand.

This may mean that:

- The tasks planned for learners are different and planned according to the individual needs of the learners.

- Alternatively, the same tasks will have different learning outcomes, depending on the individual needs of the learner. For example, some learners may require more time to complete a task than others.

- There may be different levels of support for learners. Some may be working independently and others may need more one-to-one support, or support from a teaching assistant or additional learning resources.

- The different questioning techniques you use will reflect individual learner needs. In some cases to ensure success, you may need to restrict nominated questions for some learners to the recall of knowledge or facts. However for other learners, you could use questions that are more challenging, develop higher level thinking skills and require a level of analysis or evaluation.

- The planned tasks can be achieved by using peer support in which peers can support or improve the development of each other.

Most teachers do not have the luxury of working with learners on a one-to-one basis. If you did, then differentiation would not be an issue. You would develop the learning experience based only on the needs of your one learner. However, to ensure a differentiated approach in group sessions, you have to develop the learning experience based on the needs of all your learners.

Important note

One key aspect of differentiation is that, whichever teaching strategies and methods you use, the activities should be both engaging and challenging.

With this in mind, it is useful to recognize that some activities allow for greater differentiation than others.

Those that do include:

- Any type of individual creative work
  - Mood boards
  - Posters
  - Leaflets
  - Practical hairdressing tasks.
- Experiential learning tasks which enable the opportunity to reflect and improve.
- Cooperative learning tasks in which learners work in groups in which all can take part and excel.
- Case studies
  - Expectations of learning outcomes will match the ability of the learner.
- Some questioning techniques
  - Allow waiting time for learners to reflect before they respond.
  - Use paired work so learners can discuss their answers before responding.
  - Use the principles of Blooms' Taxonomy to apply questions of different levels of ability.

- Learner presentations
  - Allow learners to work in groups, placing them with appropriate peers for mutual support and development.
- Quizzes
  - Allow learners to mark their own responses from model answers and enable time for reflection before trying any wrong answers again.

Some activities come with a health warning. As a standalone activity, the opportunity for differentiation is either non-existent, or very limited. For example:

- Watching DVDs of hairdressing techniques.
- Teacher-led learning – lectures/talks.
- Demonstrations of hairdressing techniques.
- Research for projects and assignments using reading skills.

But you can increase opportunities by:

- Watching DVDs – set a range of questions of different levels for learners to answer during and after they have observed the content of the DVD. Allow learners to stop and start the DVD at appropriate points while they practise a skill.
- Teacher-led learning – except when used in short, bite-sized pieces. Check learning by using *periodic plenary* activities.
- Demonstrations – learners may not engage, so include opportunities to involve learners in the demonstration itself. You

could do this by asking learners to tell you how you should proceed, or what the next step should be. Allow learners to actually take part in your demonstration by, for example, cutting a section, applying a foil or inserting a perm rod.

- Research using reading skills – have a range of different books and online resources set at different levels and reading abilities.

Web box

....

Activities that can be used for differentiation CPD can be downloaded from here: http://tlp.excellencegateway.org.uk/tlp/leadersandmanagers/goingforgold/b1/ index.php?i=36.

Differentiation and learning outcomes

The levels of differentiation should be clearly identifiable from your lesson plan. When writing objectives include opportunities for differentiation, such as including some or all of the following phrases:

At the end of the learning session

- All learners will be able to…
- Most learners will be able to…
- Some learners could…

Doing this will support the development of teaching and learning activities that are achievable, yet challenging, at the appropriate level for all learners in the group.

Development checklist

Visit *the Effective Teaching and Learning resource website* to download a development checklist summarizing what you have covered in Chapter 4.

CHAPTER 5

Assessment methods and techniques

Well, what does 'good' mean anyway...?

John Searle (b. 1932) US Philosopher

INTRODUCTION

This chapter will look at three different types of assessment. They are initial assessment, formative assessment and summative assessment. There are certain types of assessment that you have to do if you are delivering a nationally recognized qualification, which is usually controlled by an awarding organization. In this case the purpose of the assessment is to confirm that a learner has achieved the required standard for certification and is known as summative assessment. It is a summing up of the learner's achievements. There is another type of assessment which is also focused on learning outcomes, but in addition, helps learners to identify what they can do well and what they can improve. This assessment is formative assessment and is a way of informing current and future learning achievements by providing feedback to the learner. However, before either of these types of assessment can take place, you have to know the starting point of your learner. This can be identified through initial assessment. This chapter will explore the underlying principles of assessment to support effective teaching and learning.

CHAPTER LEARNING OBJECTIVES

This chapter will support the development of:

....

- Enhanced knowledge of Individual Learning Plans
- Greater focus on initial and ongoing assessment
- Application of assessment for learning techniques
- Increased understanding of the requirements for the delivery and assessment of hairdressing qualifications

Why assess?

Assessment is an important part of effective teaching and learning as it reflects learning achievements. Therefore, to ensure that learners have an enjoyable learning experience, it is important that any negativity about assessment is removed.

Positive assessment experiences stem from ensuring learners are following the right learning programme for them. To meet this criteria the programme should match the personal and aspirational needs of the learner, while at the same time provide challenging, yet achievable, learning outcomes. There is little point placing a learner on a programme that is academically too hard or for which they have insufficient aptitude, as they are unlikely to achieve. At the same time, placing a learner on a programme in which they fail to develop their intellect or skills can be demotivating, particularly if they feel they are repeating previous learning.

Recording the results of assessment

One key and critical factor about assessment is sharing the results. On completion of any assessment, learners need to know how well they have done. Providing constructive and helpful feedback will inform the learner what they can do well, and where they may require some further support.

Important note
Learners who do really well with tasks or knowledge need to have a clear understanding of why the results were good, so they replicate the results again. And they still need to know how they can further improve.

One way to record results of assessment and records of feedback can be in an Individual Learning Plan (ILP).

Individual Learning Plan

An Individual Learning Plan is a document which will chart and follow the learner from the beginning to the end of a learning programme. The type of document in which information about the learner is stored can vary immensely. Information about the learner may be scattered across a range of different documents, paper-based or electronic, which is acceptable, as long as the documents and the information they contain are comprehensively linked. Sometimes all the information is kept on a single document and all teachers within the organization will use the same template. In this case, while the document template may be the same for all, the content for learners, even on the same programme, will be individual. ILPs are documents which are developed in partnership with the learner and their teacher, and if applicable, their employer.

A good and effective Individual Learning Plan will include, for example:

- An outline of the learner's starting point—recognition of existing achievements, experience, skills and aspirations.
- An outline of the learner journey from start to exit, including progression routes.
- The expected learning outcomes of the programme.
- Planned dates for scheduled reviews of progress.
- Targets that are negotiated, timely, challenging yet achievable for the short, medium and long-term future.

- Review and evaluation of targets met.
- Details of support provided, effectiveness and evaluation of support.

Important note

> The best ILPs will be used as working documents, with detailed records which are continually updated with information related to the individual's learning, achievements, targets, assessment and support.

ILPs can also be used to document the implementation and evaluation of support that is identified through the effective use of **assessment for learning**. This type of continuous assessment provides opportunities to identify the individualized support a learner may require to successfully complete their learning outcomes or programme. You will find more information about assessment for learning in this chapter.

Initial assessment

Effective initial assessment will provide a whole, rounded and full picture of the learner and their learning needs. Without this you will be unable to place the right learner in the right programme. This means a programme that will meet their needs and interests, as well as their aspirations.

Important note

> All inspection frameworks in the UK include the requirement for inspectors to make judgements about the appropriateness of the initial advice and guidance given to learners at the start of, during and on exit of their programmes.

With effective initial assessment you will have:

- a range of diagnostic information about the learner relating to their knowledge and skills that might include literacy and numeracy, their chosen qualifications and how they like to learn.

- knowledge that will support the allocation of an appropriate learning programme for the learner.
- confirmation that the learning programme is pitched at the correct level of the learner to suit their current and future aspirations.
- the tools to identify and implement the support a learner may require to achieve their learning outcomes.

The term *initial assessment* might indicate that this type of assessment is only completed in the initial stages of a learning programme. While this is true and this type of assessment is carried out at the beginning of learning programmes, it should also be viewed as *ongoing assessment*. Each time a learner receives feedback, completes a review or existing support is evaluated, new initial assessment findings will be identified. Learning needs are not static, they change over a period of time and, therefore, ongoing assessment of those needs should take place.

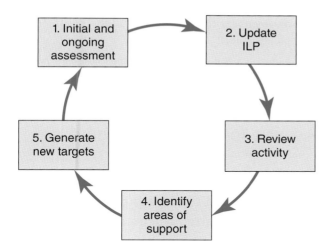

Types of initial assessment

Initial assessment often includes the following:

- An assessment of the level of literacy and numeracy at which the learner functions.
- The current and potential level of vocational, practical and technical skills related to the planned learning programme.

- Any barriers to learning related to, for example:

    - Learning needs
    - Social needs
    - Physiological needs
    - Physical needs.

- Preferred learning styles.
- Psychometric analysis.

Initial assessment will help to identify general learning needs. It will also help decisions about which level of programme is most suitable for learners. Finally, initial assessment will help to identify support that needs to be in place for a successful outcome.

Web box

....

A very helpful booklet about initial assessment for the hairdressing industry can be found here: http://www.habia.org/uploads/Initial_Assessment_-_Feb_2006.pdf.

The booklet takes you through all aspects of the various techniques that can be used for initial assessment. In addition, it can be used as a tool for reflecting on your current practice.

Initial and ongoing assessment for literacy and numeracy skills

....

Knowing the level of language, literacy and numeracy of your learners is critical for the development of individualized learning programmes and for the identification of any support that may be required. Almost all government funded learning programmes include a requirement for learners to continue with and improve their development of skills for literacy and numeracy. Judgements about the development of such skills are included in all inspection frameworks for the UK.

There are a wide range of diagnostic tools which will identify the level of literacy and numeracy at which the learner functions. Most will also identify the areas of support that are required.

Web box

··

You can find a wide range of diagnostic tool kits for various levels of literacy, numeracy and for dyslexia on the Excellence Gateway website: http://rwp. excellencegateway.org.uk/Diagnostic%20Assessment/.

Web box

··

A useful publication relating to diagnostic testing of literacy and numeracy skills can be found here: http://sflip.excellencegateway.org.uk/pdf/4.2sflguidance_3.pdf.

In addition to the use of diagnostic tools, learners may also have documentary evidence of their achievements for literacy and numeracy. For example, they may have achieved relevant qualifications in schools, colleges or through work-based learning programmes. Such achievements should be recognized and learning programmes individualized to support the further development of their literacy and numeracy skills at a higher level.

Initial and ongoing assessment for vocational, practical and technical skills

··

Learners often begin programmes with a host of experience, with some being directly related to hairdressing. They may have been employed or worked at weekends and in their holidays in relevant job roles. Some, having just left school, may have completed a vocationally related qualification which underpins the main learning aims of the programme to which they are hoping to progress.

Initial assessment can be used to identify the skills and/or knowledge the learner currently has. Knowing what this is will enable you to develop a truly individualized learning programme. Learners will be able to begin learning at their own starting point, thus preventing repetition of things they can already do. Furthermore, they will progress more quickly through their programme, maintaining interest and motivation.

Important note

Recognizing existing learning is known as accreditation of prior learning or APL. Prior learning can also include experiential learning, experience or certificated learning, so you may see acronyms to describe such recognition such as APEL, APCL and APCEL.

One way of gathering initial assessment evidence related to skill or knowledge development is by asking learners to self-assess using a skill (or knowledge) scan. This can be completed by providing a list of skills and/or knowledge required for some or all the planned learning programme. Learners will then assess how well they can perform such skills or already have knowledge about a given subject.

Online reference document

You can download an example skill scan from *the Effective Teaching and Learning resource website: Chapter 5.*

Web box

You can develop skill or knowledge scans for yourself. The questions for self-assessment are based on the National Occupational Standards for hairdressing and can be found here:
http://www .habia.org/index.php?page=1551,1626,1551.

Initial and ongoing assessment to identify barriers to learning

Barriers to learning that can be identified through initial assessment can be related to any of the following:

- *Additional learning needs*. Using a range of initial assessment tools, you can identify the level of literacy and numeracy at which the learner functions. Following which, you can then provide appropriate support to enable them to develop and progress. Some learners may have dyslexia, dyspraxia or dyscalculia, in which case, more specialized initial assessment will be required to enable appropriate support to be put in place.

- *Additional social needs*. Interviews, one-to-one discussions and external agency reports will help to identify any learning support that may be required for learners with social problems, such as financial, home or family issues.

- *Additional psychological needs*. Some learners have emotional or behavioural issues that can be a barrier for learning. These issues may not be apparent in the early days of a programme of learning, hence the importance of ongoing rather than just initial assessment. Where evidence is available at the beginning of a learning programme, it is likely to be seen in the form of reports from schools or external agencies.

- *Additional physical needs*. Some learners may be faced with long-term, or persistent and frequent short-term illness, while others may have physical impairments that may be a barrier for learning. Interviews, one-to-one discussions and external agency reports may provide an indication of the support that may be required for a success completion of the learning programme.

You can read more about barriers to learning in Chapter 3 on pages 68–69.

Initial and ongoing assessment to identify preferred learning styles

It is useful to identify how learners prefer to learn at the beginning of a learning programme. While research suggests that teachers should not place too much importance on learning styles as the sole basis for lesson planning, it is useful to know about some of the preferred learning styles. Recognizing a range of different learning styles will certainly support the development of varied and interesting approaches for the delivery of topics. You will find more information about preferred learning styles in Chapter 2.

Initial and ongoing assessment for psychometric analysis

One aspect of psychometric testing can provide an indication of personality traits. Having an insight into these traits can support effective teaching and learning, particularly when using team work as a teaching and learning method, or for team building exercises. Placing learners appropriately in teams will support effective teaching and learning. For example, if all learners in the team are leaders, very little learning will take place, as each will be competing for ownership of the task. At the same time, if the team is made up of those who lack drive and determination, very little learning is likely to take place. Effective teams will have a balance of personalities, skills and abilities. Personality traits can be identified by the completion of commercially-available psychometric tests. However, while these are always available for teachers to use, observations of learners can often indicate the more overt personality traits which may be a barrier to learning. For example, learners who demonstrate an introvert character may not learn well within groups with peers who are not sensitive to their reticent nature.

Web box

Information about one of many different types of personality testing for team roles can be found here: www.belbin.com/.

Web box

Belbin tests are available for young people. Information can be found here: http://www.belbin.com/rte.asp?id=40.

Formative assessment and assessment for learning

Formative assessment is the assessment that is used to prepare learners for their final or summative assessment. To be most effective, formative assessment must take place continuously, not just at the end of a topic or unit. Through continuous formative assessment, the teacher and the learner can identify what has been learned and if necessary, the teacher can adjust their teaching strategies and methods to provide additional support for the learner.

A powerful example of formative assessment is *assessment for learning*. Assessment for learning is a motivating tool for improving learning outcomes. It is a mechanism to combine formative assessment, in which useful information can be gathered about the readiness of the learner to be summatively assessed, and an opportunity for learners to self-assess to test their own understanding and plan where to go next. Assessment for learning is not the recognition of teacher-led learner achievement by scoring, grading, ranking or classifying learners by comparing their results against predetermined criteria, or by comparing their outcomes to that of other learners. Instead, the learner takes responsibility for assessing their own learning.

Important note

The one defining key feature of assessment for learning is that constructive, timely and useful feedback about how to improve is the central theme to the assessment activity. There is evidence to support the fact that where effective assessment for learning is used, standards of attainment are increased.

RESEARCH ACTIVITY

Paul Black and Dylan Wiliam's review of 580 research projects on effective assessment are outlined in the publication *'Inside the Black Box'* (1998). They conclude that teacher-led delivery fails to allow sufficient time for learners to reflect on new learning and that returning work that is marked and graded without providing comments about how learning can be improved is demotivating, particularly if the grades are low. The low marks only serve to reinforce a sense of failure. Black and Wiliam show that by providing more opportunities to self-assess work during the learning session, with clear and informative feedback, learners are motivated and learning increases. Read the booklet for further information and make a list of ways to encourage learners to self-assess their work constructively.

Web box

You can access further information about Dylan Wiliam and his work here:
http://www.dylanwiliam.net/.

Web box

A useful site for information about assessment is that for the Association of Achievement and Improvement through assessment: http://www.aaia.org.uk/.

It can be shown that attainment is raised when learners understand:

1 ***What the learning aim is***. This can be achieved by sharing the learning outcomes with learners at the beginning of a topic, learning activity or assessment. In addition, learners have to understand the criteria for achieving the learning aims.

2 ***How they are going to achieve their learning aim***. In the first place, learners need to recognize where they are in terms of their learning and in relation to where they have to be. They have to know how much of a gap they have to close. The closing of the gap can be achieved by appropriate and learner-centred tasks and activities in which learners are actively involved and are able to evidence their learning. This can be achieved through whole class, peer and self-directed study.

3 ***How to get to where they need to be***. This can be achieved by
providing clear, constructive and supportive feedback about what
has been achieved and what can be improved to move learning
forward. This feedback can be provided by the teacher and through
peer and self-evaluation. It is vital for learners to understand how
they can improve. As a result of the assessment feedback the
teacher can make any adjustments to accommodate the
improvements that need to be made.

Important note

*One major difference about this type of assessment is that it is not an activity that is added
onto the end of the lesson, topic or learning programme. It is an integral part of effective
teaching and learning and occurs continuously. Assessment for learning recognizes where
learners are at any given point in a teaching and learning session, or within a whole learning
programme. It identifies what learners can do and where they might need support. The
support provided occurs when teachers change their teaching and learning methods to keep
their learners on track.*

Web box

You can see some really interesting, short video clips about many aspects of
  assessment by Dylan Wiliam here: http://www.journeytoexcellence.org.uk/videos/
  expertspeakers/assessmentstrategiesdylanwiliam.asp.

Benefits of assessment for learning

By using assessment for learning you will help to prevent some of the
worst aspects of teaching and learning. For example, you will avoid
teacher-led delivery because you have to 'hand over' some responsibility
for learning to learners. You will avoid using closed questions. Instead,
the questioning techniques you will use are designed to develop higher
level thinking skills. You will avoid the over reliance on summative
assessment, in which you may not know that a learner is failing until it
is too late, because you will be continuously assessing what learners
know (or not). You will avoid demoralizing learners as you won't be
marking using grades, pass or fail. Instead you will be using supportive
dialogue and be providing helpful, individualized instruction. In addition

you will be able to adapt your methods of delivery to help the learner succeed. You will prevent classroom management issues as you will be ensuring learners are actively engaged in learning with a focus on how they learn, as an individual.

Applying assessment for learning techniques

To be most effective, assessment for learning needs to become part and parcel of your everyday teaching and learning, planning and delivery. By using assessment for learning techniques you are supporting and managing the process of teaching and learning.

There are hundreds of different ways that you can use assessment for learning at the beginning, through the main body of the teaching and learning session, and during the plenary session.

For example, assessment for learning activities for hairdressing can be:

● Questioning techniques

● Games and activities for individuals, pairs, teams and groups

● Self and peer assessment and evaluation for work completed on blocks and clients

● Setting and marking assessments

Here are just a few...

Applying assessment for learning using questioning techniques

The use and effectiveness of questioning can sometimes be overlooked. It is a powerful way to gain instant feedback about learning that will benefit the teacher and the learner. As with other teaching and learning techniques, using a wide range of different questioning techniques is more likely to motivate and engage learners.

Like other aspects of teaching and learning, questions need to be carefully planned to ensure the correct level of challenge. By using Bloom's

Taxonomy you can develop a range of questions with different degrees of difficulty about the same topic. More able learners can be further stretched by asking questions that require them to analyze or evaluate.

RESEARCH ACTIVITY

In Chapter 3 there is an activity related to Bloom's Taxonomy on page 57. You can apply the principles of the Chapter 3 activity to the development of questioning techniques. To do so you will devise a range of questions, from those requiring the simplest level of response to those that require a more complex level of response. This will result in the development and demonstration by the learner of higher level thinking skills.

Open questions A most commonly used questioning technique usually begins with words such as what, why, how, tell me, describe, explain... Using this style of question enables you to explore the depth of learner understanding or it can provide information about their opinions or feelings. To be most effective, open questions should be ***directed or nominated questions***. This means that you ask the question to a particular, named person. However, when using this type of questioning technique, once a learner has responded to a question, they may then sit back expecting that others in the group will, from then on, be asked questions. To prevent this, you can use the '*go-around cup*' technique.

Online reference document

You can download information about using the *'go around cup'* from *the Effective Teaching and Learning resource website: Chapter 5.*

Using the word 'might' in a question can be quite powerful. If you ask *what **might be** the result of applying a violet based toner on hair that is too yellow,* it infers that there may be more than one answer to the question, thus developing the reasoning skills of the learner.

Writing questions Learners could write their own questions. This technique will help with self-assessed identification of areas they are unsure of. Following this activity the teacher can adapt the session to ensure all such areas are clearly explained. This technique can also be used as a plenary activity and the questions can form the basis of the next session, linking previous learning to new.

Learners devising questions Ask learners to devise questions based on a learning topic that can be given to their peers.

Learners asking questions Learners could ask questions to the teacher, the group or to peers. If the questions are directed to the teacher, the question should be repeated and the question paraphrased. By doing so you will ensure that others in the group understand the question. Once you have done this, you can use the question asked by one learner by 'bouncing' it to another learner.

Bouncing questions This is redirecting questions from one person to another in the group. This will increase collaborative learning in which one learner gains some information from another before the question is bounced on. For example, Sam answers by saying *x, y and z about a, b and c.* You can then bounce the question to Joel by asking 'Sam said *x, y and z about a, b and c, why do you think y is better than c?*' Once you have received a response you could then bounce the question again, this time to Aamina by asking *'compare the importance that Joel places on y with those that Sam mentioned about x...'* Each time you bounce the question, you are gaining more information about the depth of understanding within the group.

Probing or extending questions This type of questioning technique supports learners to link new learning with previous learning and to develop higher level thinking skills.

For example, based on Bloom's Taxonomy, you might ask:

Which toner would you apply to pre-lightened hair that is too yellow? The response requires the **recall** of knowledge. Once you have received a response of 'violet', you could then ask the same learner to *explain the effects of a blue-based toner.* This question requires a response relating to **application** of knowledge. You could then probe further by asking *how much more effective would Brand X toner be over that of Brand Y?* This requires the learner to provide an **evaluative** response. With each question, you are developing learning as well as being able to confirm the depth and level of understanding of the learner.

Wait time Wait time is waiting for a few seconds after you have asked a question before accepting an answer from learners. If you fail to wait, some learners who instantly shout out the answer are in fact preventing the development of those who require a little more time to formulate their response. How long you wait will depend on the type of question you might ask. Recall questions require less waiting time than questions in which you are asking learners to evaluate. Wait time can be anything from 3 to 10 seconds.

Articulated answers Ask a question and allow some silent thinking time for up to one minute. Then pair learners and allow them to share their thoughts before divulging their combined, articulated response with the rest of the group.

Sharing thoughts When you have received an answer to a question, ask the rest of the group what they think to the answer provided.

Group answers Following a question allow learners the opportunity to devise their answer in a group. This will develop the skills of reasoning and negotiating when agreeing the answer.

Explicit reasoning Use questioning to turn what could be a recall answer into something more challenging. For example, instead of asking *which colour toner is used to counteract excessive yellow?*, ask *why is violet used for colour correction?*

Applying assessment for learning using self and peer assessment and evaluation

Self and peer *assessment* is about what the learner has learned, self and peer *evaluation* is how the learner has learned. Learners could be asked to assess and evaluate their own learning, or assess and evaluate the learning of peers. By doing so, they will be able to identify what they know and have done well, and you will be able to identify any support that may be required to improve future learning.

Two stars and a wish This commonly used technique can be used for both self and peer assessment or evaluation. Learners make two positive comments or judgements about their own or peers work, and one comment or judgement concerning something about the work that could be improved. The technique could be contextualized for hairdressing learners. Try using the phrase 'two GHDs (good hair days) and one restyle'.

Online reference document

You can download a template for this assessment for learning technique from *the Effective Teaching and Learning resource website: Chapter 5.*

The card used for the assessment or evaluation activity can be laminated and completed by learners using dry markers. Then the card can be re-used.

Reflective log Learners could complete a reflective diary outlining their learning achievement. The log could be linked with Individual Learning Plans and target setting.

How much, how little and now what? This self-assessment activity can be introduced as a starter activity and completed as a plenary. Learners begin the session by stating how much they already know about a given topic (***how much***). Then they state areas they are unsure of (***how little***). At the end of the activity they state areas for which they require further information (***now what?***)

Online reference document

You can download a template for this assessment for learning technique from *the Effective Teaching and Learning resource website: Chapter 5.*

KWL A variation of how much, how little, now what? Ask learners to complete three columns to reflect what they **K**now, what they **W**ant to know and what they have **L**earned. A fourth column can be added to ask, how will I learn? The activity can be used in groups, in paired work or individually.

Online reference document

You can download a template for this assessment for learning technique from *the Effective Teaching and Learning resource website: Chapter 5.*

Three, two, one Learners state *three* things they have learned and devise *two* questions they need more information about in relation to the topic. Then they have to sum up their learning session with *one* key word. This activity provides a great deal of information for the teacher. It confirms what has been understood and allows the opportunity to adapt teaching for future sessions in order to provide appropriate support for areas that have not been understood.

Online reference document

You can download an example activity for this assessment for learning activity from *the Effective Teaching and Learning resource website: Chapter 5.*

Applying assessment for learning using games and activities

Games and learner-centred activities are effective ways of captivating the interest of learners. By using a range of different games and activities you are more likely to make learning and assessment memorable.

Traffic lights or RAG cards (red, amber and green) This commonly used, but simple and very effective technique, can be used for many different purposes. Learners have three different coloured cards, red, amber and green (RAG). When asked, learners hold up a red card to indicate they do not understand. An amber card indicates that they may need some support and a green card signifies that they completely understand. The cards can be used as a starter activity, during the teaching and learning session to confirm understanding, or as a plenary activity. They can be used for both self and peer assessment. They can also be used as the basis for a learning conversation. You can read more about learning conversations in Chapter 4 on pages 94–96. Chapter 6, page 115, provides additional information about use of RAG cards as a tool for effective evaluation.

Thumbs up This is a variation of traffic light cards. Use thumbs up, thumbs level and thumbs down for learners to signify if they understand, may need some support, or don't understand.

Online reference document

You can download a template for this assessment for learning technique from *the Effective Teaching and Learning resource website: Chapter 5.*

Aeroplanes Ask learners to write a comment, question or query on a piece of A4 paper. Then fold the paper into an aeroplane and send to the other side of the room for a peer to answer the question, comment or query.

Tell me more Pair learners, or divide into teams. One side has to recall something they remember and the other side must respond with further information.

Carousel Split the group into two. One group stands in a circle with their backs to each other, facing outwards. The second group stands in a second circle facing one member of the first group in the inner circle. Learners on the inside have questions about the topic on laminated sheets. They ask one question to the person opposite, note the answer and make a judgement if they are right or wrong. The learners in the outer circle then move round one, and the process is repeated.

Online reference document

You can download an example activity for this assessment for learning activity from *the Effective Teaching and Learning resource website: Chapter 5.*

Splat the answers Split the group into pairs or very small teams. Place answers to questions on post it notes, paper or cards. Place the answers on the wall. Ask the question and then learners have to 'splat' the answer by placing their hand over the correct response.

> **Online reference document**
>
> You can download an example activity for this assessment for learning activity from *the Effective Teaching and Learning resource website: Chapter 5.*

Grand prix Learners are given a set of questions, which are all the same, but written in a different order. The first team or person to answer is the winner of the grand prix.

> **Online reference document**
>
> You can download a template for the thumbs up activity from *the Effective Teaching and Learning resource website: Chapter 5.*

Applying assessment for learning using setting and marking assessments

The timing for assessment setting can be crucial. Leaving assessment until the very end of a topic can be too late to identify those who may need more support to achieve their learning outcomes. By setting a mid-topic assessment you will enable more time for learners to reflect on learning to date and for any necessary support to be put in place.

Marking without grading Work can be marked without giving a grade or mark. Grading work can be demoralizing for learners. Sometimes learners only focus on the grade or mark and fail to look at comments. They may be disappointed to receive a 'credit' when they were expecting a 'distinction'. Marking with comments only will allow learners to instantly see what they have done well. Effective comment only marking will indicate how the learner can improve.

Providing examples of good work Sharing the learning outcomes is an important aspect of assessment for learning. When setting tasks, show learners what a good example of the learning outcome is so they know the standard they are aiming for. As an extension to this activity you could ask learners to evaluate why the work is good. This can be done with learners working individually, or in pairs.

Self or peer marking Work completed could be marked by the learner, or you ask peers to mark each other's work using the marking criteria. By doing this activity learners are more likely to acknowledge where learning has been successful. Work marked by peers is very effective as, once the work is returned, the owner of the work will be checking that marking has been carried out correctly. This again will help to identify where learning has been effective and where support is required to achieve the learning outcomes.

Share the learning outcomes Effective learning is more likely to take place when learners know what they have to achieve. This is more likely to happen if aims and objectives are outlined and displayed at the beginning of the teaching and learning session, and evaluated at the end. This can be linked to *session target setting*. When sharing the aims and objectives, set targets for attainment. These targets can be individualized to meet the needs of all learners in the group.

Redrafting Following feedback allow time for learners to redraft their work so you can provide further support.

Continuous commenting Allow learners to make comments about your comments. Use a marking template with space for your comments and that of the learners, and if appropriate, employers. You could then comment on the learner's comments.

Setting and answering own questions Ask learners to set and answer their own questions to confirm understanding of a given topic. The activity can be expanded by asking learners to devise their own marking scheme to accompany the questions. The questions can also be given to peers who can mark their own answers with the marking scheme devised by their colleague.

Feedback sandwiches Provide feedback to learners by starting and finishing with positive aspects of their work, slotting the area for improvements between the two positive comments.

Agreeing what is good Ask learners to confirm what is good about their work. This will support the understanding that they have taken your comments on board.

Taking assessment for learning further

The techniques for assessment for learning covered in this chapter are just the tip of the iceberg. The methods you can use are only limited by your own imagination. Many good and experienced teachers freely share their thoughts and ideas on teacher community websites.

Web box

One of the best websites for accessing shared information is TES
Resources. Many of the ideas on the site can be contextualized for any subject: http://www.tes.co.uk/teaching-resource/Assessment-For-Learning-Toolkit-6020165/.

 RESEARCH ACTIVITY

Geoff Petty is a renowned and respected author of books for teachers. His book *Evidence Based Teaching* will give you many more ideas for the implementation of effective assessment for learning.

Web box

You can find out more about Geoff Petty and his work from his website: http://www.geoffpetty.com/.

RESEARCH ACTIVITY

When you visit the Geoff Petty site, research another type of assessment he calls '*medal and mission*'. The *medal* is information about the learner's good work and how it is important to tell learners why and how they have achieved good work. The *mission* is the information the learner needs about the improvements that need to be made – and how they can be improved. Investigate this type of assessment and see how you can weave it into your own assessment practice.

Summative assessment and assessment *of* learning

Assessment *of* learning is a method of assessment in which a judgement is made against a set criteria or national standard. The assessment is a summing up of the learner's achievements. Sometimes the achievements are graded, or learners are ranked according to how well (or not) they have performed. Learners may have to take an exam, meet national criteria relating to competencies, or assessment judgements may be made through continuous assessment or course work. Those learners that have performed to the agreed standard will be recognized, usually in the form of a certificate.

Important note

In hairdressing, job ready qualifications such as NVQs require the learner to be competent. This means they are not graded, but they either pass or are 'not yet competent'. Therefore, 'competence' would mean that the learner has sufficient knowledge and skills to be able to perform the given task at any time, under any circumstances.

Developing summative assessment is mostly, but not always, the responsibility of an awarding organization and as a teacher, you will carry out the assessment on behalf of the awarding organization.

Qualifications for the hairdressing industry

The qualifications for the hairdressing industry in which a form of summative assessment is used form into two groups. They are:

- Vocational Related Qualifications (VRQs).
- National Vocational Qualifications or Scottish Vocational Qualifications (NVQs/SVQs).

Both types of qualifications are based on the National Occupational Standards (NOS). NVQs/SVQs will closely match the NOS while VRQs only need to relate to them.

Appropriateness of qualifications

During the initial assessment process, your meeting and interviews with learners will help to identify the type of qualification that will be most appropriate to meet their needs, interests and aspirations. It is important to have the right learner on the right programme. All inspection frameworks in the UK include the requirement for inspectors to make judgement about the appropriateness of the initial advice and guidance given to learners at the start of their programmes.

Hairdressing qualifications are designed as:

- Preparation for work qualifications–VRQs
- Job ready qualifications–NNQs/SVQs

Preparation for work qualifications (VRQs) are frequently used for delivering training to learners of school age (14–19) with an interest in hairdressing. At the end of this type of qualification, learners are not considered to be occupationally competent. VRQs are also used for continuing professional development (CPD) for individuals already occupationally qualified but who would like to take a qualification in a new technical skill area. The methods of assessment for VRQs are different for all awarding organizations. Some VRQ assessment will be based on skill and knowledge, while for others there is a bias towards the knowledge aspects. Some awarding organizations will expect learners to carry out assessments on real people while others accept evidence derived from skills demonstrated on a modelling block.

Job ready qualifications (NVQ/SVQs) are based on competence. They are the qualifications used in hairdressing apprenticeships and have been the main hairdressing qualifications used for 16–19 year olds, as well as adult learners training for the hairdressing industry. There are many different awarding organizations that offer NVQ/SVQs, and the assessment is the same for all of them. Awarding organizations must ensure that learning providers offering their qualifications meet the assessment strategy requirements set by Habia.

Web box

....

Habia is the Sector Skills Body (SSB) for the Hairdressing and Beauty Industry. Habia is also part of SkillsActive, the Sector Skills Council (SSC) for Sport and Leisure. You can download the assessment strategy to which all awarding organizations must subscribe from: http://www.habia.org/index.php?page=404,479,404,1.

Important note

There are separate assessment strategies for the delivery of European and African-type hair qualifications. The assessment strategy sets out the requirements to ensure the rigour and consistency of assessment procedures,and that those involved in the assessment process remain highly qualified, experienced and technically up to date.

In addition, the assessment strategy includes:

Mandatory requirements

- Performance in the Workplace and Use of Simulation
- Approach to Achieving Greater External Quality Control of Assessment
- Requirements for the Occupational Expertise of External Verifiers, Internal Verifiers and Assessors
- Appendices in which there is information relating to:
  - Realistic Working Environment requirements
  - Summary of where simulated activities may be used

- Areas within the Hairdressing National Occupational Standards (NOS) for which mandatory question papers must be developed

- Occupational expertise requirements for hairdressing assessors and verifiers

- Requirements for continuing professional development (CPD) for hairdressing assessors and verifiers

- Nationally agreed maximum service times for hairdressing NVQ/SVQ assessment purposes.

Awarding Organizations are responsible for ensuring that those delivering hairdressing qualifications must comply with the Habia criteria for both the ***Realistic Learning Environment*** (RLE) and the ***Realistic Working Environment*** (RWE).

Realistic Learning Environment (RLE) criteria for VRQ delivery

1 A Realistic Learning Environment must be established in schools, colleges, private training providers and other premises approved for the delivery and assessment of preparation for work type qualifications that contain a practical skills element.

2 Approved centres must develop realistic management procedures that incorporate a ***salon image*** and a sales and marketing policy.

3 The space per working area must conform to health and safety legislation and commercial practice.

4 The range of services, professional products, tools, materials and equipment must be up-to-date and available for use. They must enable learners to meet the requirements of the relevant preparation for work qualification.

5 A reception area where models are greeted and general enquiries and appointments can be made by telephone or in person must be available. Ideally, industry-specific ICT facilities should also be

provided. The reception area must also include a payment facility (artificial money may be used).

6 The RLE must take full account of any by-laws, legislation or local authority requirements that have been set down in relation to the type of work that is being carried out there.

7 Learners must work in a professional manner taking into account industry establishment requirements such as:

  (i)   appearance and dress code
  (ii)   personal conduct
  (iii) client service, hospitality and communication
  (iv)   hygiene
  (v)   reliability
  (vi)   punctuality

Realistic Working Environment (RWE) criteria for NVQ/SVQ delivery

As the Standards Setting Body for the Hairdressing and Beauty sectors, Habia is responsible for defining what constitutes a 'Realistic Working Environment' (RWE). Habia has set down the following criteria for the assessment location. This will ensure that all learners are being assessed against the National Occupational Standards in a realistic working environment when not in an actual, commercial workplace.

The following criteria must be included as part of centre approval and must be confirmed as being met during the first external verification visit. The criteria must then continue to be met on every subsequent visit. This will ensure that learners are able to meet commercial needs in the workplace.

1 Assessment centres must develop realistic management procedures that incorporate a 'salon image'* and sales and marketing policy to attract the type and number of clients needed to ensure that the requirements of the National Occupational Standards can be achieved.

2 All assessments must be carried out under realistic commercial pressures and on paying clients and not other candidates within the same group. Clients should vary in age and hair condition so that the requirements of the National Occupational Standards can be achieved.

3 All services that are carried out should be completed in a commercially acceptable timescale. Maximum service times for particular, critical services have been developed by Habia for each Hairdressing NVQ/SVQ and are detailed in Appendix 1F. These times should be used for assessment purposes.

4 Learners must be able to achieve a realistic volume of work.

5 The space per working area conforms to health and safety legislation and commercial practice.

6 The range of services, professional products, tools, materials and equipment must be up-to-date and available for use. They must enable learners to meet the requirements of the National Occupational Standards.

7 A reception area where clients are greeted and general enquiries and appointments can be made by telephone, or in person, must be available. The reception area must also include a payment facility.

8 A retail facility must be provided with products that relate to the clients' needs and the services offered.

---

*The use of the word 'salon' is not intended to deny access to the hairdressing qualification if you deliver hairdressing services in other locations (for example, hospitals, care centres etc.). It refers to any place where professional hairdressing services are carried out. However, the location must meet health and safety requirements for hairdressing.

9 The RWE must take full account of any by-laws, legislation or local authority requirements that have been set down in relation to the type of work that is being carried out there.

10 Learners must work in a professional manner taking into account establishment requirements such as:

   (i)   appearance and dress code
   (ii) personal conduct
   (iii) hygiene
   (iv) reliability
   (v)   punctuality

11 Learners are given workplace responsibilities to enable them to meet the requirements of the National Occupational Standards.

Development checklist

Visit the online site to download a development checklist summarizing what you have covered in Chapter 5.

CHAPTER 6
Successful starts and evaluative ends

Every beginning has an end and every end has a new beginning.

Santosh Kalwar, born 1982 – Nepalese author

INTRODUCTION

This chapter focuses on the significance of the beginning and the end of teaching and learning sessions. With a clear beginning and end to learning, you will be able to confirm that learners are making progress. The start of teaching and learning sessions is a crucial point in which you have the opportunity to link previous learning with that planned for your session, and in addition to this, to confirm learners' current understanding. The end of the teaching and learning session provides opportunities for reflection and learner-centred feedback and evaluation to inform future learning sessions. The start and end of teaching and learning should refer to all learning objectives and be carefully planned, delivered and learner-centred.

As well as evaluating learners' work and progress, it is also important to evaluate your own teaching practice. You need to be sure that the teaching and learning strategies you are implementing are effective. They must support learning, develop learners personally, socially and economically, allow them to make progress and meet their needs and interests. Using information in this chapter you can self-assess your effectiveness against some of the aspects that measure the impact of excellent teaching and learning.

CHAPTER LEARNING OBJECTIVES
This chapter will support the development of:

....

- Recognizing the importance of an effective and clear start to a teaching and learning session
- Implementing ideas for a range of starter activities
- Recognizing the importance of effective evaluation on completion of a teaching and learning session
- Implementing ideas for a range of plenary activities
- Self-assessment to confirm the extent of learning by learners at the start, during and on completion of a teaching and learning session

The importance of successful starts for teaching and learning

Effective learning can only begin when learners are settled. Wherever possible, it is useful to have the same preparation routine for learners to adhere to, so they can quickly prepare for their teaching and learning session. The minutes prior to, and at the extreme start of a teaching and learning session, will set the scene for the remainder. If learners are not engaged at the very start, they are more likely to disengage during the main session.

For example, in a practical class:

Learners should:

- Arrive punctually with the correct tools and equipment.
- Know the routine for storing coats and bags to ensure a safe working environment.
- Be prepared with appropriate salon footwear and clothing.
- Set up their work stations as soon as they arrive in the salon.
- Sterilize tools and equipment on arrival.
- Have their log books and assessment criteria ready for formative and summative assessment.
- Check the appointment schedule and prepare appropriate equipment and client records.

You should:

- Be consistent in your expectations for session preparation.
- Be fully prepared and ready to begin the learning session on time with an outline of the learning objectives.
- Have sufficient and appropriate clients or alternative resources to challenge and meet the needs and interests of learners.
- Provide appropriate support for all learners and ensure learners and (if appropriate) additional teachers have a clear role and responsibilities.
- Allocate appropriate clients to maximize learning and assessment opportunities.
- Have alternative, meaningful, constructive and planned tasks ready and prepared should clients be late or fail to arrive for appointments.
- Have planned contingency plans should there be too many or too few clients.
- Ensure learners know the routine for arranging formative and summative assessment.
- Ensure learners begin tasks efficiently without losing learning time.
- Appropriately challenge learners who are late and ensure a seamless transition into their learning.

For example, for theory subjects:

Learners should:

- Know the routine for storing coats and bags to ensure a safe working environment.
- Know their routine for seating positions.
- Arrive punctually with the correct materials, books, equipment, etc.

You should:

- Be consistent with your expectations for session preparation.
- Carefully think about the seating plan to support learning and good behaviour.

- Ensure learners go to their own seats, even if you plan to do paired and group work later.
- Settle learners quickly so learning can begin without interruption
- Have predictable tasks and start the teaching and learning session in the same way to provide structure. **Note** – this does not mean that you will use the same activities.
- Have a constructive, work-related warm up activity for early arriving learners to complete while waiting for the class to begin. For example a crossword, hangman, anagram or key word activity that is linked to previous learning.

Web box

....

A useful website for making anagrams is: http://www.easypeasy.com/anagrams/. For example, by entering the word 'sebaceous gland' the anagram generator can provide anagrams such as *Cleanse Soda Bug*.

The importance of evaluative plenaries for teaching and learning

While the first few minutes at the start of a teaching and learning session are important, you must not underestimate the importance of the last few at the end of a teaching and learning session. This is an opportunity to consolidate learning and succinctly pull together all the themes of the entire session.

At the end of the session, you need to know:

- That your learners have grasped the key concepts of the session and that they have met the learning objectives.
- That the teaching and learning strategies and methods used were successful (or not), so you can adapt learning for future learning sessions.

- If there are gaps in learning so you can provide the appropriate support.
- That learners have made progress relative to their individual starting points.
- *What* your learners have learned and *how* they have learned it.

One key consideration of a plenary session is that to be able to evaluate learning effectively, the learners must be able to tell *you* what they have learned – not you tell *them*. Therefore, learner-centred evaluation activities are required.

Periodic plenaries

In Chapter 5 we looked at assessment for learning. Using assessment for learning techniques will enable you to gain and provide instant feedback about learning that will benefit the learner and the teacher. To maximize the impact of assessment for learning you can introduce a *periodic plenary* at any time during a teaching and learning session. The periodic plenary can be used to bring the learners together to focus for a very short period on the learning outcomes at that moment in time. The periodic plenary provides an opportunity to ensure all learners are, at that moment, on track for meeting their individual targets. If they are not, you should have sufficient time in the remainder of the session to adapt your plans or provide additional and individualized support – while you still have the opportunity.

Periodic plenaries also provide a vehicle to share good practice. For example, in a practical hairdressing session a learner may have completed a very good or particularly creative technique. So that other learners can see and share in the good practice demonstrated, stop all learning, and gather all learners together to talk about the work demonstrated. By doing so, in addition to the feedback you provide to the individual learner, all learners can be involved in peer evaluation.

So, don't be afraid to stop a session at any point and share the learning outcomes again. Waiting until the end could be too late...

Benefits of using activities as session starters and for evaluation

There are numerous benefits for choosing to use a range of activities before you begin with the main body of learning, and on completion. It is important to recap on previous learning and to set the scene for the planned learning for the session. You also need to know that the learning aims have been met. This is commonly done by the use of questions. However, sometimes questioning techniques can be limiting. And, depending on the type of questioning techniques used, they can be time consuming. Plus, you may not be able to make a judgement about the learning outcomes for all the learners in the group. However, by using quick, focused activities you will gain more information about the learners' current levels of understanding in a relatively short length of time.

Starter and plenary activities will:

- Engage learners from the very beginning of the session and pull learning themes together at the end of the session.
- Give you the opportunity to introduce an immediate level of challenge that will set the scene for the remainder of the session.
- Develop the expectation that all learners have to work, think and participate in the session.
- Encourage learner interaction from the beginning and through to the end of the session.
- Provide an alternative to asking questions. Furthermore, the start and end of the session can be different each time, preventing predictability of teaching and learning methods and therefore, complacency amongst learners.

Starter and plenary activities

In Chapter 4 you will find information about a teaching and learning 'menu' on pages 103–106. For an enticing and appetizing learning experience learners need a 'starter', a 'main course' and a 'dessert'. In other words, an activity to begin learning (starter), activities to meet the main learning objectives (main course) and a plenary activity (dessert) which will allow both you and learners to sum up the learning experience, to reflect and to plan for future learning.

Although the starter or plenary activities may be short, planning for them is every bit as important as planning the main learning objectives. The same 'rules' apply. As with all other activities, these must also meet the needs and interests of all learners. Therefore, the aspects of all the chapters in this book will relate to starter and plenary activities. For example:

1 **Communication** must be appropriate for the starter or plenary activity. Teachers must be clear about what they expect learners to do. Learners must be able to articulate what they know, and importantly, from this information the teacher will be able to identify what they don't know. Starter and plenary activities should be short, brisk (but not rushed) and focused. Learners should be told how long they have to complete the task. You could use a timer as an auditory or visual reminder. The lesson plan example in the downloads section of Chapter 3 provides an illustration of how to use time to plan your lessons.

Web box

....

Use the search facility for a range of different timers at: http://www.learning resources.co.uk or try http://www.brightideasteaching.co.uk/Classroom-Management/Sand-Timers.

2 You need to know **how your learners learn** and build on their preferred learning styles, allowing for the development of other skills during the starter and plenary activities.

3 You need to **plan** the starter or plenary activity and use the activity to recap previous learning, assess what learners know and provide the stepping stones for the new planned activities in your session. Remember to use naturally occurring opportunities to embed planned literacy and numeracy skills as well as promotion of equality and diversity within the curriculum.

4 Use a range of **different strategies and methods** for your starter or plenary activities so learners do not become complacent and anticipate the teaching and learning session. Remember to allow for differentiation.

5 Use your starter or plenary activities to **assess** learners' current levels of understanding and to use the learning outcomes to identify support and to plan future learning.

Web box

....

Teachers are very generous about sharing their ideas for resources. One of the best resources sites for starters and plenaries is TES Resources. For example, you can download 120 starter and plenary ideas through this link: http://www.tes.co.uk/teaching-resource/The-Starter-Generator-6020073/.

Applying starter and plenary activities

Using a range of different activities is important to keep learners interested and engaged. Some activities can be used as a discrete starter or a plenary activity, or they can be used as either. Other activities can be used to start the session, and then the same type of activity used again at the end of the teaching and learning session. Some activities that are used as assessment for learning can also be used as starter and plenary activities. See Chapter 5 for more information and ideas.

There are hundreds of different activities you can use, which include:

- Mind bubbles or if you have the appropriate software, mind mapping
- Listing
- Labelling
- Taboo™
- Timed explanation
- Questioning
- True or false

- RAG cards (traffic lights)
- Number/letter cards
- Matching card games
- Bingo
- Crosswords
- Word search quiz
- Walls of words

Mind bubbles

This type of activity is based on mind mapping. It is a quick activity which can be carried out individually, in pairs or in small groups. The activity can be used to recap existing knowledge or to link previous learning with new. It is a good activity to develop 'constructs' and to reinforce key words and terms.

> **Online reference document**
>
> You can download examples of different starter activities based on mind bubbles from *the Effective Teaching and Learning resource website: Chapter 6.*

Listing

Learners are asked to list everything they can remember about the previous teaching and learning session. They can do this by using bullet points, spidergrams, mind mapping or write in sentences. Give a set time (use a timer if you have one). When the time allowed has elapsed, ask learners to share their responses with a partner. Allow a short time for discussion and then ask learners to share their findings with the rest of the group. Have a pre-prepared list of the key words they should have identified. Allow learners time to self mark their work and check how many key aspects they remembered. Mini whiteboards (or laminated paper) are a good resource to have for this type of activity as they can be used again. You will be able to identify any significant gaps in learning through the completion of this activity.

Labelling

Provide diagrams for items such as hair, skin, hair growth cycle, colour molecules, perming and neutralizing processes for learners to label. Provide the correct answers and use peer marking to confirm results of activity. You will be able to identify any significant gaps in learning through the completion of this activity.

Online reference document

You can download examples of diagrams for labelling from *the Effective Teaching and Learning resource website: Chapter 6.*

Taboo™

This is a game-based activity which is useful for recapping previous knowledge or, alternatively, confirming the learners' understanding of new knowledge. Split learners into teams of three.

Team roles:

- One team member will describe a hairdressing skill, word, process, or action without using the words that are taboo and must not be said. This person is known as the *describer*.

- One team member tries to guess what the hairdressing skill, word, process or action is. This person is known as the guesser.

- One team member ensures that the 'taboo' words are not used. This person is known as the checker.

A card which contains hairdressing-related skills, words, processes, or an action is given to the describer. The guesser has to listen to the describer and identify the hairdressing skill, word, process, or action. The describer must not say any of the Taboo^{TM} words. The checker has a copy of the card and must stop the game if any of the Taboo^{TM} words are used.

You will need two cards for each word and sufficient cards for the entire group. Once the hairdressing skill, word, process, or action has been identified by the guesser, team members play a different role.

Online reference document

You can download examples of Taboo^{TM} type games from *the Effective Teaching and Learning resource website: Chapter 6.*

Timed explanation

You will need two 'scripts' which contain succinct key points about two aspects of current or previous learning sessions. Learners are paired and one learner has one of the 'scripts'. The second learner is given a set length of time in which they have to say as many things as they can remember about the particular topic of the session. The learner with the script ticks off the key words or items mentioned. The activity is repeated with the second script of key points. You will be able to identify any significant gaps in learning through the completion of this activity.

Questioning

Using questions is a frequently used technique to begin and end a session and to confirm learner progress and understanding. To be most effective, it is important to vary the types of questions you use. In Chapter 5 you will find information about using a range of questions as assessment for learning.

The questioning techniques include the following types:

- Open
- Directed or nominated
- Writing questions
- Devising questions
- Learners asking questions
- Bouncing
- Probing or extending
- Wait time
- Articulated
- Sharing thoughts
- Group answers
- Explicit reasoning

Cube questions An additional tool that can be used for enhancing questioning techniques, and useful for plenaries, is using a cube that is rolled revealing a range of different statements. On each side of the cube is a statement, from which learners have to say how they have achieved the revealed statement during their learning session. The cube can be related to literacy and numeracy skills, personal learning and thinking skills, or even to Bloom's Taxonomy. By demonstrating where they have applied a range of different skills, learners' achievements will be reinforced and the embedding of, for example, literacy and numeracy skills, will be strengthened.

Online reference document

You can download directions and example cubes that can be used for developing and enhancing your questioning techniques from *the Effective Teaching and Learning resource website: Chapter 6.*

True or false

This game, which can be used as a starter or plenary activity, requires learners to hold up one of two cards. One card says 'true' and one 'false'. The teacher makes a statement and learners have to state if the statement is true or false. To ensure that learners are not influenced by their peers, ask learners to hold up their responses all at the same time. You can vary this activity by using questioning techniques to discuss the correct answer when a false answer is given. See more about questioning techniques in Chapter 5.

Online reference document

You can download examples of true or false statements from *the Effective Teaching and Learning resource website: Chapter 6.*

RAG cards (traffic lights)

Red, amber and green cards (RAG) can be used for so many different purposes. Learners have three different coloured cards, red, amber and green (RAG). When asked, learners hold up a red card to indicate they do not understand. An amber card would indicate that they may need some support and a green card would signify that they completely understand. The cards can be used as a starter activity, during the teaching and learning session to confirm understanding, or as a plenary activity. They can be used for both self and peer assessment. They can also be used as the basis for a learning conversation. You can read more about learning conversations in Chapter 4. In addition you can use RAG cards to identify attitudes or barriers to learning. For example, at the beginning of a learning session, learners hold up the card which best reflects their attitude to learning on that day or for that session. If they are happy, have no issues or barriers, then they would hold up a green card. Holding a red card would signify that they have some issues that could be a temporary barrier to learning. It is important if a red card is held up, that the learner is taken to one side at a convenient time to identify support that will be required to help the learner during the teaching and learning session.

Primary and secondary colour cards A plenary activity useful for recapping understanding of the colour star, and based on the principles of RAG cards, are cards of the primary and secondary colours. Learners are given six cards of red, yellow and blue, and of green, orange and purple. The teacher asks learners to display the primary colours or the secondary colours. Then they ask learners to display the colour that is made from two, named primary colours. Again, it is useful to ask learners to reveal their cards at the same time to prevent them being influenced by other learners.

Number/letter cards

This activity is similar to the true–false activity in that learners will have a series of cards with 1, 2, 3, or 4 or a, b, c, or d. Use multiple choice questions for learners to respond to with 1, 2, 3, or 4 or a, b, c, or d. To ensure that learners are not influenced by their peers, ask learners to hold up their responses all at the same time. You can vary this activity by using questioning techniques to discuss and to challenge why the answer is correct, or how it can be improved.

Matching and sorting card games

Cards can be used for a variety of different activities. One example is dominos. You can find some examples of domino games that can be used as a start or plenary activity in Chapter 2 on pages 31–32. Other card matching games that can be used are:

- Matching definitions
- Identifying the correct order of processes
- Sorting items into groups

To make the matching and sorting games more challenging, you could add spurious cards which do not fit into any of the categories. If you choose to do this, you should tell learners at the beginning of the activity.

Online reference document

You can download examples of matching and sorting card games from *the Effective Teaching and Learning resource website: Chapter 6.*

Bingo

This is a quick and easy game for learners to play at the beginning and end of teaching and learning sessions. Play the game to confirm understanding of key words used during the session.

You can provide learners with laminated boards with a grid, in which they can choose their own key words to write in from a given list. Alternatively, you can generate Bingo cards for them to complete. The teacher then states a definition and the learner locates the matching word on their bingo card and crosses off the word. The usual Bingo rules apply for the winner – a full house, complete lines up, down or diagonally.

Web box

A useful site for the generation of Bingo cards that you can devise from your own word lists and clues can be found here: http://saksena.net/partygames/bingo/ You can opt in or out of the 'free square' choice.

Online reference document

You can download an example of a Bingo game from *the Effective Teaching and Learning resource website: Chapter 6.*

Crosswords

This is a great way of confirming knowledge and understanding. You can use the clues as a means of recall, or you can make them more cryptic to develop higher level thinking skills. You could ask learners to generate their own crosswords for peers to complete. There is a plethora of crossword generators freely available on the Internet.

Web box

....

Try any of the following crossword generators for your puzzles. This one allows
you to input as many as 20 clues:
http://www.crosswordpuzzlegames.com/create.html
You can save the puzzles you generate for up to two months on this site:
http://www.armoredpenguin.com/crossword/
You can share your crossword clues on this site:
http://worksheets.theteacherscorner.net/make-your-own/crossword/crossword-puzzle-maker.php.

Word search quiz

....

Although learners may enjoy them, word searches as a standalone
activity are not particularly good for confirming a level of
understanding. However, the activity can be enhanced by asking
learners to find the answers to clues in the same way they would for a
crossword puzzle.

Web box

....

You can make word searches using any of the following sites:
http://www.armoredpenguin.com/wordsearch/
http://tools.atozteacherstuff.com/word-search-maker/
http://www.teachers-direct.co.uk/resources/wordsearches/.

Walls of words

....

The use of 'walls' makes a good starter or evaluation activity, and the
only resources required are flip chart paper, markers and sticky notes.
The notes posted by learners will confirm learning and provide
information to inform future teaching and learning sessions. Some
'wall' ideas are:

Great wall of ideas This can be used as a plenary activity. The flip
chart paper can be painted to look like a wall, or you can draw blocks
to look like bricks. At the end of the session, ask learners to write an
idea for future learning and post on the wall before they leave.

Wherever possible, use their ideas to ensure learning is meeting their needs and interests.

Wonder wall This can be used as a starter, plenary, or ongoing activity. The wonder wall flip chart paper is made available for learners to post any questions they might be 'wondering' about related to the teaching and learning session. The teacher can refer to the questions at any time in order to answer them immediately, or to include in plans for future sessions.

Graffiti wall Pieces of flip chart paper are available for learners to write on at any time throughout the session. Learners are asked to write their responses and thoughts about the teaching and learning topic, to draw pictures or ask questions. The more colourful the better – so provide lots of coloured markers. Use the findings to provide further feedback or plan future teaching and learning sessions.

Graffiti walls can also be developed by displaying a number of mood boards based on the teaching and learning objectives.

Teacher or self-evaluation

When sessions are graded by your peers, or by outside observers or by inspectors, the focus of any grade is on the *learning* that takes place, not on the *teacher*. Teachers can be good performers. They can entertain their learners and learners may enjoy the session. However, unless learners have learned independently or through collaboration with others, met the learning objectives, made progress relative to their starting points, and produced work of a standard that is better than the minimum required by their qualification, no matter how entertaining the teacher is, the grade would be less than good.

There are no magic formulas and there are no set criteria about what makes a learning session better than good. But, there are some typical and tangible learning-centered aspects of a teaching and learning session which support learner progression, and that you can make part of your every day teaching and learning sessions.

Online reference document

You can download and complete a self-evaluation exercise to identify the level of success for *learning* that has taken place in your session from *the Effective Teaching and Learning resource website: Chapter 6.*

RESEARCH ACTIVITY

All government bodies with responsibility for assuring the quality of learning providers will carry out inspections based on the framework requirements of their own nation. Investigate the judgment criteria for teaching and learning for your own inspection body.

England

http://www.ofsted.gov.uk/resources/common-inspection-framework-for-further-education-and-skills-2012

Scotland

http://www.educationscotland.gov.uk/inspectionandreview/

Wales

http://www.estyn.gov.uk/english/inspection/

Northern Ireland

http://www.etini.gov.uk/index.htm

Development checklist

Visit *the Effective Teaching and Learning resource website* to download a development checklist summarizing what you have covered in Chapter 6.

Activity reference

Chapter	Activity name	Topic area	Activity type	Purpose and application	Preparation
2	Dominos	Cutting consultation	Game	Starter Plenary Supporting cognitivism – reinforcing learning	√√√
2	Cutting text	Cutting hair	Questions	Supporting behaviourism – providing reward	√
2	Cutting case study	Cutting hair	Case study	Supporting constructivism – making 'constructs'	√
2	Go around cup	n/a	n/a	Questioning techniques	√√
2	Images for hair cutting	Cutting	Practical	Supporting humanism – providing opportunities for self-motivation	√
4	Numbered heads together	Advice and consultation	Multiple choice	Cooperative learning	√√
4	Jigsaw	Colour	Game	Cooperative learning	√√√
4	Jigsaw	Colour tests	Game	Cooperative learning	√√√

Chapter	Activity name	Topic area	Activity type	Purpose and application	Preparation
4	Jigsaw	Hair growth	Game	Cooperative learning	√√√
4	Jigsaw	Perming	Game	Cooperative learning	√√√
4	Numbered heads together	Colouring	Case study	Cooperative learning	√√
4	Team, pair, solo	Cutting	Recap and research	Cooperative learning	√
4	Team, pair, solo	Hair tests	Recap and research	Cooperative learning	√
4	Team, pair, solo	pH scale	Recap and research	Cooperative learning	√
4	Team, pair, solo	Massage	Recap and research	Cooperative learning	√
4	Team, pair, solo	Selling	Recap and research	Cooperative learning	√
4	Team, pair, solo	Hair condition	Recap and research	Cooperative learning	√
4	Team, pair, solo	Colour products	Recap and research	Cooperative learning	√
4	Think, pair, share	Disease and disorder	Recap and research	Cooperative learning	√
4	Think, pair, share	Health and safety	Recap and research	Cooperative learning	√
4	Think, pair, share	Hair growth cycle	Recap and research	Cooperative learning	√
4	Think, pair, share	Cutting tools	Recap and research	Cooperative learning	√

Chapter	Activity name	Topic area	Activity type	Purpose and application	Preparation
4	Think, pair, share	Blow drying	Recap and research	Cooperative learning	√
4	Think, pair, share	Face shapes	Recap and research	Cooperative learning	√
4	Experiential learning colour	Colouring	Practical and reflection	Experiential learning	√
4	Experiential learning consultation	Advise and consult	Practical and reflection	Experiential learning	√
4	Experiential learning styling	Styling hair	Practical and reflection	Experiential learning	√
4	Learning conversation concept	All areas	Conversational learning	Learning conversation – supporting target setting and individualized learning	√
4	Modelling consultation	Consultation	Demonstra-tion, practice and reflection	Modelling	√
4	Modelling cutting	Cutting	Demonstra-tion, practice and reflection	Modelling	√
4	Modelling cutting portfolio	Cutting portfolio	Demonstra-tion, practice and reflection	Modelling	√
4	Modelling promote products and services	Promote products and services	Demonstra-tion, practice and reflection	Modelling	√
4	Multi-sensory colouring	Colouring – highlights	Demonstra-tion followed by practice	Multi-sensory learning	√√√

Chapter	Activity name	Topic area	Activity type	Purpose and application	Preparation
4	Multi-sensory cutting	Cutting	Demonstration followed by practice	Multi-sensory learning	√√√
4	Multi-sensory plaiting	Plaiting	Demonstration followed by practice	Multi-sensory learning	√√√
4	Relating practice to theory colour correction	Colour correction	Case study	Relating practice to theory	√√
4	Relating theory to practice basic colour	Basic colouring	Case study	Relating theory to practice	√√
4	Technology colouring	Colour theory	QR Code treasure hunt	Technology	√√√
4	Technology cutting	Cutting theory	QR Code treasure hunt	Technology	√√√
4	Technology perming	Perming theory	QR Code treasure hunt	Technology	√√√
5	Go-around cup	All areas	Questions	Supports nominated questioning techniques	√
5	How much, how little, now what?	All areas	Assessment for learning	Starter Plenary	√
5	Carousel	Hair and skin structure	Assessment for learning	Revision	√
5	Initial self-assessment skill scan	Shampoo and condition hair and scalp	Assessment for learning	Self assessment	√√√
5	KWL	All areas	Assessment for learning	Starter Plenary	√

Chapter	Activity name	Topic area	Activity type	Purpose and application	Preparation
5	Three-two-one	All areas	Assessment for learning	Plenary	√
5	Thumbs up	All areas	Assessment for learning	Plenary and periodic plenary	√
5	Two GHDs and one restyle	All areas	Assessment for learning	Plenary and periodic plenary	√
6	Bingo	Hair structure	Assessment for learning	Starter Plenary	√√
6	Matching and sorting definitions	Hair and skin structure	Assessment for learning	Starter Plenary	√
6	Matching and sorting – grouping	Styling	Assessment for learning	Starter Plenary	√√
6	Matching and sorting – grouping	Facial shapes and hairstyling	Assessment for learning	Starter Plenary	√√
6	Matching and sorting – order	Promote products and services	Assessment for learning	Starter Plenary	√√
6	Mind bubble colouring	Hair testing – colouring	Assessment for learning	Starter Plenary	√
6	Mind bubble – cutting	Cutting	Assessment for learning	Starter Plenary	√
6	Mind bubble – hairstyling	Hairstyling – facial shapes	Assessment for learning	Starter Plenary	√
6	Questions using Bloom's cube	All areas	Assessment for learning Questions	Starter Plenary	√√√
6	Questions using comms cube	Communication	Questions	Starter Plenary	√√√

Chapter	Activity name	Topic area	Activity type	Purpose and application	Preparation
6	Questions using number cube	Numeracy	Questions	Starter Plenary	√√√
6	Questions using PLTS cube	Personal, learning and thinking skills	Questions	Starter Plenary	√√√
6	Taboo™ colouring	Colouring	Game	Starter Plenary	√
6	Taboo™ hair growth cycle	Hair growth cycle	Game	Starter Plenary	√
6	Taboo™ hair structure	Hair structure	Game	Starter Plenary	√
6	Taboo™ perming	Perming	Game	Starter Plenary	√
6	True false colouring	Colouring	Game	Starter Plenary	√
6	True false hair and skin structure	Colouring	Game	Starter Plenary	√
6	True false styling	Colouring	Game	Starter Plenary	√

Glossary

Additional learning needs Learners may require additional support, such as literacy, numeracy or vocational skills.

Additional physical needs Learners may require additional support if they have long term, or persistent and frequent short term illness. Some may need additional support because of sensory impairments such as eyesight or hearing.

Additional psychological needs Learners may require additional support for emotional or behavioural issues which distract them from learning.

Additional social needs Learners may require additional support because they may be unemployed, with family problems, are carers or single parents, or are without a permanent home.

Assessment A judgement or the quality of a learning outcome.

Assessment for learning Constructive, timely and useful feedback about learning outcomes and how the learner can improve is the central theme to the assessment activity.

Assessment of learning Method of assessment in which a judgement is made against a set criteria or national standard.

Behaviourism A theory of learning relating to the learning of new behaviours.

Bloom's Taxonomy Describes three different categories of learning activities. The categories are *knowledge, skills* and *attitude*.

Cognitivism A theory of learning relating to thinking and the development of cognitive skills

Constructivism A theory of learning in which new information or concepts are computed and connected to existing information or concepts.

Cross-cultural communication An understanding of effectively communicating across a range of different cultures.

Curriculum The topics that will be covered in the learning programme.

Curriculum plan The order in which topics in a learning programme will be covered.

Differentiation Using effective planning for teaching and learning, including strategies and methods that will meet the individual needs of all learners.

Dyslexia Frequently described as a learning *difference*, rather than a learning *disability*, in which learners may have problems with their fluency of reading and writing.

Equality, Diversity and Inclusion (EDI) Support for organizations and individuals to improve their understanding, knowledge, confidence and practices in equality, diversity, inclusion and community development.

Evaluation Analysis of the effectiveness of teaching and learning outcomes.

Every Child Matters (ECM) Multi-agency approach to sharing information to help children achieve and be a success.

Experiential learning Learning by experience.

Formative assessment The assessment that is used to prepare learners for their final or summative assessment.

Go-around cup (also known as the dialogue cup) A technique for structuring nominated or direct questions using a behaviourist approach by rewarding learners with a praise word they respond to. Can be used when applying the teaching method of learning conversations.

Humanism A theory of learning in which learners have a degree of choice and where they can be empowered and take responsibility for their own learning.

Individual Learning Plan A document which will chart and follow the progress and learning support of the learner from the beginning to the end of a learning programme.

Informative speech The main form of transmitting communicated information.

Initial assessment A method of assessment used to determine the starting point of a learner at any given time throughout a learning programme.

Learning aims The general, overall context or content for a lesson or learning programme.

Learning cycle For example, learners plan, complete and review a task.

Learning objectives The measurable targets of learning outcomes for a lesson or learning programme.

Learning styles For example visual, auditory, reading/writing and kinaesthetic learning.

Lesson plan The method used to organize the detail in which a topic will be taught and assessed within a given time.

Multiple intelligences Howard Gardner's (1983) theories on how learners learn.

Occupational standards The benchmark for qualifications outlining the expected level of competence at different levels.

Periodic plenary An evaluation of learning that can take place at any time during, rather than just at the end of a teaching and learning session.

Personal Learning and Thinking Skills (PLTS) A framework for describing the qualities and skills needed for success in learning and life.

Persuasive speech A communication approach used to influence learners to accept a particular position.

Preferred learning How learners prefer to learn.

Reflective listening Used to confirm the meaning of what is being said by repeating back what you think you have heard.

Scheme of work A working document used to plan the long term, overarching aspects of the curriculum in a logical and coherent order for teaching and learning.

Sector Skill Body The organization responsible for the development of standards for a particular sector.

Specifications (programme specifications) An outline of the expected learning outcomes by describing them through modules or units related to a particular subject.

Summative assessment The summing up or the final assessment of a topic or subject.

Teaching method The 'tool' used to deliver and meet the specific learning outcomes.

Teaching strategy The teaching strategy is based on the number and interaction of learners and teachers within a given environment.

VARK An acronym for visual, auditory, reading and kinaesthetic learning.

Bibliography

Beere J. (2011). *The Perfect Ofsted Lesson*. Carmarthen: Crown House

Black P. et al. (2005). Putting ideas into practice. In: Black P. et al *Assessment for Learning*. Maidenhead: Open University Press. 30–57

Black P. et al (2005). *Assessment for Learning – Putting it into Practice*. Berkshire: Open University Press

Black P. Wiliam D. (1998). *Inside the Black Box*. London: GL Assessment Limited. 1–21

Brown K. (2009). *Classroom Starters and Plenaries*. London: Continuum International Publishing Group

Daines J. et al (2006). *Adult Learning Adult Teaching*. 4th ed. GB: Continuing Education Press

Department for Education and Skills (now DfE) – *Working Together to Safeguard Children*. Guidance Document 2006

Dix P. (2012). Putting the TA in team work. *tespro*. 35 (25 May), 8–9

Eggen P. Kauchak D. (1992). *Educational Psychology Windows on Classrooms*. 8th ed. London: Pearson. 181–185

Evans D. (2012). Making the most of mixed ability. *tespro*. 33 (11 May), 4–7

Evans D. (2012). Find your voice and look after it. *tespro*. 37 (8 June), 4–7

Gershon M. contributor to TES Resources http://www.tes.co.uk/teaching-resources/

Goldsbro J. White E. (2007). *The Cutting Book*. London: Thomson

Goldsbro J. White E. (2009). Basic Communication. In: Goldsbro J. White E. *The Official Guide to the Diploma in Hair and Beauty Studies*. Andover: Cengage Learning EMEA. 215

Gravells A. Simpson S. (2011). *Planning and Enabling Learning in the Lifelong Learning Sector*. 2nd ed. Exeter: Learning Matters Ltd

Hodgson D. (2009). *The Little Book of Inspirational Teaching Activities*. Carmarthen: Crown House Publishing

Keeling D. (2002). *Rocket up your Class*. Carmarthen: Crown House Publishing

Laurillard D. (2002) *Rethinking University Teaching: a framework for the effective use of educational technology* 2nd ed. London: Routledge Falmer

Lucey C. (2012). Why AfL is not a passing fad. *tespro*. 1 (16 September), 4–7

Moore A. (2007). *Teaching and Learning Pedagogy, Curriculum and Culture*. Oxon/New York: Routledge

Mortimore T. (2006). *Dyslexia and learning style*. London: Whurr Publishers Ltd. 93–110

Ofsted Report – *Safeguarding Best Practice*, 2011

Parker P. (2012). Finding a pattern to follow. *tespro*. 35 (25 May), 4–7

Petty G. (2008). Initial and diagnostic assessment. In: Petty G. *Teaching Today*. 4th ed. Cheltenham: Nelson Thornes. 529–545

Petty G. (2008). Assessment. In: Petty G. *Teaching Today*. 4th ed. Cheltenham: Nelson Thornes. 479–513

Petty G. (2009). Feedback methods: assessment for learning. In: Petty G. *Evidence Based Teaching*. 2nd ed. Cheltenham: Nelson Thornes. 246–276

Pritchard A. (2011). *Ways of Learning*. 2nd ed. Oxon/New York: Routledge

Rafe 1990 – 'First tell them what you're going to tell them, then you tell them. Then you tell them what you told them'

Scales P. (2010). Assessment for learning. In: Scales P. *Teaching in the lifelong learning sector*. Berkshire: Open University Press. 173–199

Stewart W. (2012). Think you've implemented assessment for learning? *TES*. 13 July. 24

Wallace S. (2010). *Teaching, Tutoring and Training*. Exeter: Learning Matters Ltd

Wiliam D. (2007). Assessment for learning: why, what and how? In: Wiliam D *Assessment for Learning: why, what and how?* London: Institute of Education. 1–40

Claude S. Warren W. (1949) *The Mathematical Theory of Communication*. Illinois: The University of Illinois Press

Web research

Atherton J. S. (2011) *Learning and Teaching; Knowles' andragogy: an angle on adult learning* [Online: UK] retrieved 16 December 2011 from http://www.learningandteaching.info/learning/knowlesa.htm

Atherton J. S. (2011) *Learning and Teaching; Experiential Learning* [Online: UK] retrieved 26 June 2012 from http://www.learningandteaching.info/learning/experience.htm

Atherton J. S. (2011) *Learning and Teaching; Aspects of Cognitive Learning Theory* [Online: UK] retrieved 26 June 2012 from http://www.learningandteaching.info/learning/aspects_cog.htm

Atherton J. S. (2011) *Learning and Teaching; Humanistic approaches to learning* [Online: UK] retrieved 26 June 2012 from http://www.learningandteaching.info/learning/humanist.htm

Atherton J. S. (2011) *Learning and Teaching; Conversational Learning Theory; Pask and Laurillard* [Online: UK] retrieved 11 August 2012 from http://www.learningandteaching.info/learning/pask.htm

http://tlp.excellencegateway.org.uk/tlp/pedagogy/talkinteachingt/index.html - information relating to pedagogic methods included in Chapter 4

Kolb learning styles: http://www.infed.org/biblio/b-explrn.htm http://www.businessballs.com/kolblearningstyles.htmhttp://archive.excellencegateway.org.uk/page.aspx?o=152477

www.deni.gov.uk – The Department of Education for Northern Ireland information relating to teaching in Northern Ireland

www.education.gov.uk – safeguarding information

www.fepdscotland.co.uk – The Professional Development Forum Scotland

www.geoffpetty.com/evidence_based_downloads.htm – downloads for teaching and learning

www.habia.org - Habia information relating to hairdressing Sectors NVQ Assessment Strategy and CPD requirements

www.jigsaw.org/ – information relating to jigsaw learning

www.legislation.gov.uk – The Further Education Teachers Qualification (England) Regulations 2007

www.lluk.org – Lifelong learning UK (LLUK) website for Further Education sector

www.open.ac.uk – The Open University – Becoming a teacher

www.prospects.ac.uk – Association of Graduate Careers Advisory Services (AGCAS) provides career guides and information on teaching and Education

www.teachertrainingwales.org – Teacher Training and Education in Wales

www.teachinginscotland.com – Scottish Government Education Department– information relating to teaching in Scotland

Index